The Commandments
– for real – for now

'So he was there with the Lord forty days and forty nights; he neither ate bread nor drank water. And he wrote on the tablets The Words of the Covenant, The Ten Commandments.'
Exodus 34:28

Paul O'Sullivan

Sovereign World

Sovereign World Limited
P.O. Box 17
Chichester
England, PO20 6YB

ISBN 1 85240 051 X

Typeset by CRB Typesetting Services, Ely, Cambs.
Printed in England by Clays Ltd., Bungay, Suffolk

Acknowledgements

We stand on the shoulders of others to see further, and in having this book published it is a joy to acknowledge those whose shoulders I have stood upon, and have stood alongside.

Roger Waters sowed the original revelation of the progressive nature of the decalogue into my spirit in the early 1970s. He is a man who has a profound understanding of God's relationship with man and is currently busy writing material which I believe will be widely read and appreciated.

Standing beside me in putting the teaching into study form in the 1980s was Peter Carblis, my brother-in-law and an inspiring teacher of God's Word. He is the senior pastor of a large church in the central coastal district of New South Wales, Australia.

Also my dear wife who, with her discerning mind, helped to get my writing back to the heart of the message when that was needed.

Finally I thank those who read the manuscript with a critical eye, especially Pastor Hal Oxley, a senior man of God, from whose wisdom and experience I draw constantly, and for his microscopic attention to the areas that needed the tidiness required for publication.

Contents

Decalogue		7
Foreword – *Tom Marshall*		9
Chapter 1	A Law for Life	11
Chapter 2	Of, Through, and To	17
Chapter 3	The Image Makers	26
Chapter 4	Seeking of Endorsement	40
Chapter 5	Entering into Rest	51
Chapter 6	Who's the Boss?	66
Chapter 7	Live and Let Love	85
Chapter 8	Till Death (or whatever) do us Part	96
Chapter 9	Your Money or Your Life	105
Chapter 10	Tell It Like It Is	114
Chapter 11	Enough is Enough	121

The Ten Commandments
Exodus 20:1–17 (NKJV)

And God spoke all these words, saying:
2 *'I am the Lord your God, who brought you out of the land of Egypt, out of the house of bondage.*
3 *'You shall have no other gods before Me.*
4 *'You shall not make for yourself any carved image, or any likeness of anything that is heaven above, or that is in the earth beneath, or that is in the water under the earth;*
5 *you shall not bow down to them nor serve them. For I, the Lord your God, am a jealous God, visiting the iniquity of the fathers on the children to the third and fourth generations of those who hate Me,*
6 *but showing mercy to thousands, to those who love Me and keep My commandments.*
7 *'You shall not take the name of the Lord your God in vain, for the Lord will not hold him guiltless who takes His name in vain.*
8 *'Remember the Sabbath day, to keep it holy.*
9 *Six days you shall labor and do all your work,*
10 *but the seventh day is the Sabbath of the Lord your God. In it you shall do no work: you, nor your son, nor your daughter, nor your manservant, nor your maidservant, nor your cattle, nor your stranger who is within your gates.*
11 *For in six days the Lord made the heavens and the earth, the sea, and all that is in them, and rested the seventh day. Therefore the Lord blessed the Sabbath day and hallowed it.*
12 *'Honor your father and your mother, that your days may be long upon the land which the Lord your God is giving you.*

13 '*You shall not murder.*

14 '*You shall not commit adultery.*

15 '*You shall not steal.*

16 '*You shall not bear false witness against your neighbor.*

17 '*You shall not covet your neighbor's house; you shall not covet your neighbor's wife, nor his manservant, nor his maidservant, nor his ox, nor his donkey, nor anything that is your neighbor's.*'

Foreword

This book teaches in an area that is vital but very neglected in the church today, that is, ethics, or how we are meant to live in a way that is pleasing to God. We find that God has not left us in the dark as to the quality of life He requires or the means that are available to achieve it. He has given us His Son, Jesus Christ, as the model of what we are to aspire to become and He has given us His Holy Spirit to write His law on our hearts and enable us to conform to Christ's image.

It is with the second of these provisions, the law of God and specifically the expression of that law in the Ten Commandments that is dealt with here. Paul O'Sullivan underscores two essential keys to understanding the contemporary and eternal significance of the Ten Commandments. Firstly he deals with the essential unity of the law of God on which Jesus and the apostles insisted, and he shows in an interesting way, the interrelatedness of the commandments and why, if we break them in one point we are lawbreakers and in fact guilty of all. (James 2:8–11)

Secondly, and this is the main thrust of his message, he demonstrates that God has not given us a detailed set of ethical rules that fit every occasion we are likely to meet. Instead He has given us broad principles, with some specific examples to give them teeth and to get us started. Our task is to apply those principles as honestly and as creatively to the real life situations we face day by day. When we do, the law is written on our hearts and our character changes.

It is here that Paul O'Sullivan's pastor's heart shows. He takes the individual commandments, boundary rules that they are, and examines the real life implications of the principles they contain. There is a wealth of experience for pastors and counsellors to draw on and practical applications that will touch our personal lives at many points. It is not a 'treatise' on systematic theology. Neither is the Bible. Like the Bible it struggles with real life and ethical issues that overlap and are untidy, often ambiguous and rarely straightforward.

Our generation struggles with issues that are veritable moral minefields of searing difficulty and frightening complexity. The church desperately needs to think ethically, and teach ethics far more than it is doing at this moment. This book is a welcome attempt to give some markers for the ordinary Christian to find his way safely.

Tom Marshall
Sydney, Australia
October 1991

Chapter 1

A Law for Life

A Man on a Mountain

'Moses has been gone almost six weeks now, and it's been too long, far too long!' Frustration and impatience had set in to the hearts of the children of Israel. Their leader had gone up to Mt. Sinai, up amongst the clouds – Why was he up there and why for so long? – He was their link with God. If he had disappeared, then maybe this God, this 'I AM' had disappeared also.

Impatience – the cause of so many wrong decisions. So they built the idol of the golden calf and they called it 'God'. So impatient that they broke the first two commandments before they had even received them!

Then Moses came down from the mountain and saw their idolatry. He had the two stone tablets with him. There were storm clouds in his face. So he broke the two tablets of stone. How prophetic! The commandments would be broken anyway! At least the first set. He built another two tablets and these he did not break. Again, a prophetic picture of the commandments coming a second time, in another way, 1500 years later, to a new covenant people. This time written in the heart, where through grace and faith they can be fulfilled and not broken.

A Heart for Relationships

Relationship is the key value in the whole theme of the commandments, because God wants us to be fulfilled in life through relationships, both with Himself, and with one another.

We find then that the first four commandments deal with our relationship with God, and that the next six deal with our relationships with one another.

That is why the New Covenant had a promise that the law would be written *in our hearts by The Holy Spirit, a person,* who can indwell us and make alive the spirit of the law, and the standards of God's wisdom for our relationships. This can now be done on the powerful basis of love and grace, instead of legalism.

Unfortunately, the people to whom the law was given were a people devoid of spiritual understanding, whose hard hearts prevented them from knowing God's ways.

> *'Wherefore I was grieved with that generation, and said, They do always err in their heart; and they have not known my ways.'*   Hebrews 3:10 (King James)

A People in Bondage

'Not this Moses again, still trying to tell us what to do – He says it's for our own good – I suppose just like it was for "our own good" when he got our fathers into trouble forty years ago by slaying that Egyptian, and burying him in the sand – well no thanks, not this time.'

The children of Israel had been in bondage in Egypt for four hundred years, and they had lost any understanding of God, not to mention a loving God, and they certainly weren't going to trust Moses too easily. Four hundred years was a long time to go without any sermons, any prophets, any spiritual leaders, and there was as yet no such thing as a priesthood, except for the pagan Egyptian priesthood, with its harsh and cruel religion.

Law meant only one thing to them. It meant oppressive and cruel authority, depriving them of freedom, and forcing submission out of them, with stiff penalties for disobedience, and no mercy. That meant that you could not relate to a lawgiver, because he was not interested in your welfare. *'Just make more bricks.'*

Moses had a task ahead of him – how to get these people not to just relate to a *law*, but rather to relate to a loving, caring Father behind that law. A law that would restore their souls and delight the hearts of those who loved Him.

A Divine Design

God had concealed an amazing design within the structure of His ten commandments. He had designed them as a sequence of steps where success in any one commandment leads to an understanding of the next. Obedience to the first commandment gives understanding of the second commandment, and in the same way, failure in say, the sixth commandment means a lack of understanding in the fifth.

Let us look at that first example, where obedience to the first commandment gives understanding of the second. The first commandment says, '*I am the Lord your God who led you out of bondage ... you shall have no strange gods before me ...*' Now this establishes a very important fact. That is, God is to be number one in our lives. He is our God, therefore He is our creator, source of life and meaning, and the One for whom we live, above all others.

It is clear then, that if this fact is grasped and believed in, and obeyed, we would not be foolish enough to fashion another inferior god, and believe that *it* could become a source of life and provision and meaning, and for us to live for *that* god and trust in it.

But suppose we lost sight of commandment number one and were unable, through ignorance or unbelief, to trust on the one true God to be our everything, then we would have to invent something, whether it was a material image, or some kind of self image created by our imagination, that we would choose to trust in.

And so the downward path begins. We will cover this particular example further when we deal with each commandment in fuller detail. But let us look at another example already mentioned, the fifth and sixth commandments.

The fifth commandment says '*Honour your father and your mother*', and the sixth says '*Thou shalt not kill*'. So how are these related?

If we look at the personal relationships involved (remember that relationship is the key value in all the commandments), we see that commandment number five, honouring our parents, speaks about a requirement for the very first relationship we experience as human beings. Our first experience of relationships is with authority, and is a totally dependent one.

In this relationship we are being taught, in a very natural way, *to trust another person* (or usually two other persons, a mother and a father) for the needs in our life. (In a perfect world, with perfect people this trust would grow and grow, and we would trust them for wisdom and direction and instruction and correction. But we don't live in a perfect world.

The reason that this relates to the sixth commandment is found in the statement that Jesus made in the sermon on the mount, when He said *'In the law it says thou shalt not kill, but I say unto you, be not angry with your brother without cause.'* Put in simple terms – anger kills.

Anger kills relationships and it kills people. And where does anger come from? It comes from the frustration of not having our own way because of other people, and our lack of trust in other people. So by experiencing frustrations in not getting our own way as children in an imperfect world under the authority of imperfect parents, we start becoming independent, and decide to get what we want, *our way*. After all, how can we trust a mother and a father, no matter how loving, to give us exactly what *we* want?

We then carry this mistrust and independence into our lateral relationships and display the anger, the sulkiness, moodiness or aggression, or, in other words, that which *kills a relationship*. People start to get in the way of our goals and our desires for fulfilment and satisfaction.

A Circle of Growth

And now we discover another amazing principle. That is, that the growth pattern of the ten commandments takes us all the way around to commandment number ten, *and then leads us right on to commandment number one again.*

Let us take our last example one step further, into the seventh commandment – '*Thou shalt not commit adultery*'. If we have failed in commandment number six, whereby *people* are getting in the way of our goals and desires to be fulfilled and satisfied, then, as well as getting angry, moody, or whatever, we will be tempted to forsake a person. More precisely, to *forsake a relationship, even marriage*, to be satisfied and gratified in some other way, perhaps in *another relationship*. This is, of course, the spirit of adultery.

So the downward path is in fact a downward spiral. Alternatively, and in a positive sense, the upward path is an upward spiral, and spiritual growth is taking place. This growth will always take place if a person is willing to honestly admit where they are failing and go back one step and correct the response to the previous commandment, and then leap forward in revelation and faith. In fact, this book is written to help you take hold of the revelation of faith for growth in the principle contained in each commandment.

The evidence of the circular nature of the progression of the commandments is seen graphically when we get to commandment number ten and find that the next progression is to *commandment number one*!

This can be explained by the fact that the nature of the problem in commandment number ten, which is the commandment against covetousness, is that of *idolatry and discontent*. Those persons who are not content with what they have, live their lives out of coveting what someone else has, and so, the source of their fulfilment is what others have. This is a form of idolatry and is called such in the Bible (Col. 3:5).

And there we have the circle completed. The answer to this covetousness and idolatry of course, is found in commandment number one, where we acknowledge God alone as our fulfilment. This is why commandment number ten, and commandment number two (on either side of commandment number one), both deal with idolatry.

A Proper Expectation

The commandments can then be seen to serve as some kind of a map like that of a main roadway, or a railway line, where a person always knows what the next destination will be because they have passed through the last destination. As we go through the ten commandments one by one, we will see that there is a principle of growth involved in each commandment and an experience of faith that will stay with us as we apply ourselves and are obedient to the revelation that we receive at each 'stop' along the way. God intends all growth to be established on a firm basis of experience.

This means that we can be wise in our expectations and not try to grow up all at once, but be patient, letting God have His way, in His timing, and in His knowledge of our level of spiritual maturity. He takes us round and round His cycle of truths and lessons found in the commandments, and when a breakdown occurs, there is God's word, the conviction of The Holy Spirit, and our conscience, all helping us to diagnose what the problem is and what is the prescription of faith to remedy the fault.

If there comes a point of failure at some level of experience, then we find God causing us to go back to the previous commandment to see what we have overlooked in our haste, unbelief, or disobedience. As we let The Holy Spirit reveal truth to us in this way, we realise that growth becomes a function of *life* rather than of the letter, *and that this is not just some self improvement programme*. This also affords a most effective chart of diagnosis for the serious counsellor who wants to see a life transformed by the truth and power of The Holy Spirit.

Chapter 2

Of, Through, and To

The First Commandment

I am The Lord your God, who brought you out of the land of Egypt, out of the house of bondage. You shall have no other gods before Me.   Exodus 20:2–3 (RSV)

Putting God First in our Lives

This commandment is actually the be-all and end-all of the commandments. It tells us that we should look to no other person or thing than God Himself for our ultimate meaning, purpose, and fulfilment. The spirit of this commandment can be seen in the new testament scripture of Romans 11:36 (King James).

*For **of him**, and **through him**, and **to him**, are all things: to whom be glory for ever. Amen.*

If this scripture were fully understood and applied by every child of God, then there would only be need for *one* commandment, because this would fulfil all the rest. Obedience to this would mean total dependence upon God in our daily lives.

What happens however, is that we might see something as being *of God* but not do the thing *through God*, or perhaps not direct it *to God*. For instance, it may be of God, but *through us*, and unto Him.

That is why the first commandment begins a logical sequence of challenges to faith and obedience. The next commandment, which deals with the making of images, only becomes relevant when a person has not remained dependent upon God as the source and means and end of his life, and so builds for himself or looks to some other source, or finds some other means of strength that becomes a 'god' to him.

Release from Bondage

God had to release Israel from bondage before He could give them the commandments. He knew that the bondage had caused bitterness in their souls by reason of their cruel taskmasters in Egypt, and His loving response to them was one of compassion.

> *And The Lord said, 'I have surely seen the affliction of my people which are in Egypt, and have heard their cry by reason of their taskmasters; for I know their sorrows.'*
>
> Exodus 3:7 (King James)

God told Moses to tell them of His promises for them, but they were unable to respond. God's most formidable task was to convince them of His love for them, let alone *transform* them. This next passage of scripture contains the phrase 'I will' seven times. It is the pronouncement of the Mosaic covenant – a loving covenant from a loving God.

> *And I have also heard the groaning of the children of Israel, whom the Egyptians keep in bondage; and I have remembered My covenant.*
>
> *Wherefore say unto the children of Israel, I am The Lord, and **I will** bring you out from under the burdens of the Egyptians, and **I will** rid you out of their bondage, and **I will** redeem you with an outstretched arm, and with great judgements:*
>
> *And **I will** take you to me for a people, and **I will** be to you a God: and ye shall know that I am The Lord your God, which bringeth you out from under the burdens of the Egyptians.*

> *And **I will** bring you into the land, concerning which I did swear to give it to Abraham, to Isaac, and to Jacob; and **I will** give it to you for an heritage: I am The Lord.*
>
> *And Moses spake so unto the children of Israel: but they hearkened not unto Moses for anguish of spirit, and for cruel bondage.* Exodus 6:5–9 (King James)

It was only after their deliverance from Egypt, that the commandments that were meant to bless and fulfil them as a people, could be revealed. And for this fulfilment to take place, Israel had to be made mature in the knowledge of God. Being made mature in the knowledge of God takes place through a process of growth, which involves experience of personal challenge, in which the mind and heart are transformed.

We can only be transformed when we see the need for that change of heart and mind, and most people do not realise how much they need to be changed. In fact, we neither fear the challenge of change as a threat to our independence, and therefore excuse pride and sin, or we feel 'trapped' in our personality flaws, without hope of ever being changed. The commandments showed Israel the need for this change of heart and mind by revealing sin in their lives in a very practical and real way. But this was not designed to condemn them, but rather to bring them 'into the light', where God's love and forgiveness was.

The effect of this first commandment therefore was to reveal to Israel their basic sin, namely, that they *could not put God first in their lives*. God knew that this was because of their bondage of heart, and for this reason, *the promise of deliverance is tied to this commandment*.

Bondage and the Believer

> *He has delivered us from the power of darkness and translated us into the kingdom of the Son of His love.*
> Colossians 1:13

As with Israel, God has provided for the Christian a supernatural deliverance from bondage so that we can obey His commandment to put God first in our lives.

Much has been taught and discussed and applied concerning 'the deliverance ministry', and indeed, I witness the grace of God in situation after situation where the power ministry of the Holy Spirit is exercised in an ordered and authoritative way, to secure release from spiritual bondage in the believer. However, the principle that I see as the most effective means of setting a person free from spiritual captivity is that found in 2 Timothy 2:24–26.

> *And a servant of The Lord must not quarrel but be gentle to all, able to teach, patient,*
> *In humility correcting those who are in opposition, if God perhaps will grant them repentance, so that they may know the truth, and that they may come to their senses and escape the snare of the devil, having been taken captive by him to do his will.*

The greatest weapon that the devil has to keep a person in captivity, is to keep them 'in the dark' concerning their problem, or their bondage.

Let me give you an illustration concerning two people who wanted to put God first in their lives, and in their marriage. This is a true story but we will give them fictitious names – Jack and Jill.

As they sat opposite me in my office, across a coffee table (I hate using a desk), they looked at one another nervously, each trying to quietly signal the other to start first. So I thought I'd better open things up and start with the direct approach.

'How about you telling me how you see the problem, Jack.' Jack leaned forward and Jill settled back, visibly relieved.

'It's my temper – I'm sick of it – I've never been violent with Jill, but I get so mad with her, and it's happening too often. I even start getting mad when I come through the front gate … It's stupid … and I love her, but oh, I don't know, I just don't know what it is with me.'

'Anything you get especially mad about Jack?' I asked.

'It can be just about anything she says. She … well … she …'

'Go on, say it Jack. I nag,' spoke up Jill.

'I don't always call it nagging, Jill.'

'I know. Sometimes you call it worse!'

It was time for me to break in again.

'What do you call it Jill?'

'I know I'm *demanding*, and I hate myself for it, but I get so insecure and he doesn't seem to care, or even understand how I feel. And yet I know he loves me. And I love him. I know I nag him. But I've got to make him listen to me. But then he just gets mad.'

'O.K.' I said, sounding a lot more confident than I felt. 'The Lord knows exactly what you are both trying to say – He understands it all.'

They looked at me trustingly. I looked at them both and said.

'What have you said to God about all this?'

'We've confessed our sin.' – almost in unison.

Then it came to me – What sin were they confessing? – Were they merely confessing their guilt, without understanding what The Holy Spirit was trying to convict them about? – There is a big difference. I turned to Jack –

'Jack, describe what you feel about yourself, when you react to Jill.'

'Well – I feel inadequate I suppose. She makes me feel like a failure – like I've failed to love her because I haven't done enough, or, haven't done something the right way.'

'And this makes you angry?'

'Yes, angry with myself mostly, and then with Jill.'

I looked at Jill.

'We men are pretty sensitive about our egos Jill. I say this to our shame, and I'm making no excuses for Jack, but your demands, or what he calls "nagging", make him feel like a failure. Now Jill, can you tell me how you feel about yourself when you are in reaction to Jack?'

'I feel rejected and unloved.'

'O.K.' I said again, this time more confidently.

I addressed Jack again.

'What sin did you confess to The Lord, Jack?'

'Bad temper, anger, impatience.'

I turned to Jill.

'What sin did you confess Jill?'

'Nagging, demanding ...'

I looked steadily at Jack again, thinking of the words I would choose. If I said them slowly enough, maybe he'd get the revelation I was about to share with him.

'Jack, when you said you felt inadequate, when Jill nagged you, you were actually confessing your *fear of failure*. That fear is the bondage that is stopping you from loving your wife, and obeying God, or in other words, *putting God first*.

I turned to Jill, my words coming faster.

'And Jill, your *fear of rejection* is stopping you from *trusting* Jack.'

They were both looking at me intently, waiting for me to go on. I knew truth was dawning – the truth that sets free – I went on.

'Neither of you have really confessed your sin at all! – You have both been confessing what you felt guilty about. You have been "in the dark" about the real nature of your sin. Those fears have kept you both in bondage – and God wants to set you free from that bondage.' I paused. 'Jack, when Jill "nags" you, she is really saying "do you love me Jack?" because her fear of rejection makes her naturally feel unloved, even though God loves her, and so do you.' I paused again, there was faith in the room. 'And Jack, you can have victory through Christ, by choosing to love Jill and put away that fear of failure, which is simply unbelief in the grace of God, to let Christ's love flow through you.'

I began to share with them about 'the axe being laid to the root of the tree' and that they had only been dealing with the branches. We began to look in the word of God concerning 'the exchanged life of Christ' and the liberty of the Spirit that comes when we are in the light concerning our sinful nature. That they now had liberty to choose what pleased God, and were no longer captive to the devil, being taken captive by him at his will. They were both released into repentance and faith as we prayed.

What was happening was the Holy Spirit ministry of the law being written on the hearts, the New Covenant fulfilment of the Old Covenant law that revealed sin to Israel. But the New

Covenant application was accompanied by grace and faith, and the power of The Holy Spirit to appropriate the life of Christ in the experience of growth. As we go through the ten commandments, we will actually see the areas of bondage, as described above, which prevent a person from living fully in the revelation of the first commandment, that is, of, through, and to God in all things.

The New Covenant Statement

There is a scripture in the New Testament that parallels the first commandment in the Old Testament.

> *Yet for us there is only one God, The Father, of whom are all things, and we for Him; and one Lord Jesus Christ, through whom are all things, and through whom we live.*
> 1 Corinthians 8:6

In this scripture we see a fourfold principle in putting God first in our lives. These are:

1. The Fatherhood of God
As our father, God is the source of our lives. He is therefore the provider for, the protector of, and the source of love and acceptance in our lives. Many people have a distorted view of God, just as Israel had, and expect to be punished and deprived instead of cared for and blessed. To be sure, God will discipline us, but in a way consistent with His father heart of love and compassion.

If we can trustingly obey this word concerning God, and not depart from Him as Israel did, through their *'evil heart of unbelief'* (Heb. 3:12), we will find a true sense of belonging to God, and a true identity in Him, seeing all things as being of God.

2. Our Purpose in God
Our lives only have meaning as we relate to our Father God's intention in our lives (Eph. 1:3–6). This causes us to acknowledge His wisdom for our life decisions.

Obedience to this means submitting to God's absolute authority over our lives, and putting God's call and purpose first in our lives. It also means seeking God for the ways in which this call and purpose will be outworked. Then all things are unto the glory of God. This is the way Jesus related to His Father.

> *Then Jesus answered and said to them, 'Most assuredly I say to you, the Son can do nothing of Himself, but what He sees The Father do; for whatever He does, the Son also does in like manner.*
>
> *For the Father loves the Son, and shows Him all things that He Himself does; and He will show Him greater works than these, that you may marvel.'*
>
> John 5:19–20

3. The Lordship of Jesus

For Christians (unlike Israel), to whom the divinity of Christ is revealed, this commandment bears reference to Jesus.

Obedience to this means that we acknowledge that The Father has given to Jesus supreme authority, and that we submit to Him in His Lordship.

> *That at the name of Jesus every knee should bow, of those in heaven, and of those on earth, and of those under the earth,*
>
> *and that every tongue should confess that Jesus Christ is Lord, to the glory of God the Father.*
>
> Philippians 2:10–11

4. Identification with Jesus

Jesus, the Son of God, is our brother. It is through the gift of life that He has given us, that we can obey our Father and share in the inheritance He has won for us. Understanding this truth and 'laying hold' of it by faith is operating the principle of the exchanged life of Jesus Christ. He becomes our strength. He becomes our obedience to The Father, as we yield to His power within us. He changes and softens our heart to desire the thing that He would do, to perfectly please our Father.

Of, Through, and To

'I have been crucified with Christ; It is no longer I who live, but Christ lives in me; and the life which I now live in the flesh I live by faith in the Son of God, who loved me and gave Himself for me.'
Galatians 2:20

Chapter 3

The Image Makers

The Second Commandment

'You shall not make for yourself any carved image, or any likeness of anything that is in heaven above, or in the earth beneath, or that is in the water under the earth; You shall not bow down to them nor serve them. For I, The Lord your God am a jealous God ... '

Exodus 20:4

What is an Image

Our humanity craves tangible forms of things to relate to, to fix in the mind, to hang on walls, to put in frames, to make into statues, etc. The two main ingredients of an 'identity image' are, firstly, the concept of the thing as it first exists in someone's mind, and then the form of it, as it is represented in some kind of shape or form, even in an abstract form, such as an ideology, or an 'ism', like communism.

So a definition that can be given for an 'identity image' then, is: 'The representation of some special form, that gives identity to a person or group.' That is a pretty simple definition, but you will find it covers the range of image making processes that peoples' minds go through when they are seeking to find some self identity.

Remember the golden calf. That was a confused concept of what Israel thought to be God Himself. It was not meant to be *another* god. Their concept was shaped by their past experience. They fashioned what was the 'sacred cow' of Egypt, a golden calf (or golden bull). So you can see how important the form itself is in the use of an image or an ideology. Just as

26

worship was attached to the image of the golden calf, as some form of activity or behavioural response, so too, there are behaviours and attitudes attached to other 'identity images.' Take for instance communism's formalised manifesto, or humanism's formalised manifesto, which gives identity to millions of people in the world today, who deny a living Father God, from whom they can draw their identity. We will look at the mode and effect of some of these 'isms' later on.

But can you see the relationship of this commandment to the first commandment? Can you see the shift, because of unbelief and distrust, from finding identity and meaning in the one true invisible God, to grasping meaning from some tangible form, solid or abstract, that projects man's centre of being and purpose?

This is the first step of self rejection. We reject *ourselves* as objects of love from a loving, faithful God, because we reject *Him* as our creator and sustainer. Man's greatest attempt at architecture is to fashion for himself a 'self image' which he can trust and depend upon. As His efforts in building this image get greater and greater, so do his real values become more and more confused, concerning the worth of himself, and of humanity in general. And so we see abortion and euthanasia becoming acceptable forms of social control of 'emotional problems', while at the same time, the death penalty for criminal murder is abolished in the name of being 'humane'. (We will discuss the matter of the death penalty for murder when we come to the study of the sixth commandment – 'Thou shalt not kill'.)

Some Expressions of Idolatry

We have seen a couple of different forms of idolatry so far, so now let us look at what you might call 'the range' of idolatrous forms, within which most expressions of idolatry fall. We will list the following five categories.

1. Cult Idolatry
2. Religious Idolatry
3. Ideological Idolatry
4. Hero Worship
5. Self-Image Building

1. Cult Idolatry

This includes the worship of personified false gods, such as Astarte (Judges 2:13), Baal (Judges 2:13), Dagon (Judges 16:23), Molech (Lev. 18:21), and so on. Most pagan societies have (or have had) many such gods, usually represented in some form of statue or picture. This also of course, includes occultism and Satan worship in which supernatural power is ascribed to incantations, talismans (magic charms and images) and secret rituals.

I watched with interest, and some dismay recently, a television interview with the 'High priest' of a satanic cult. A television interviewer, very sincere, and very, very, serious, was mediating between the 'high priest' and a cross section of the community, some dozen people, including some Christian clergy. Also included in the community panel were victims of satanic rituals. These poor victims, one of which was a teenage girl who had been subjected to horrendous sexual abuse, and who had witnessed infanticide in rituals, were asking that the law step in and ban these types of activities. Everybody, including the interviewer, was on the Christians' side when it came to condemning the activities of the cult. But when it came to acknowledging a personal 'Satan' or 'Lucifer' let alone a personal God, nobody would own up! (except the Christians). Even the 'high priest' said that 'his Lucifer' was not personal.

He denied that 'his satanism' was involved in such illegal activities, and blamed the Christian, biblical concept of Satan for the perverted behaviour of the 'twisted' people referred to. His cult, he said, was only interested in the obtaining of total sensual gratification, without harming others. 'His Lucifer' was merely a name which was the focus for the releasing of highly motivational powers for them to do and have what they wanted and be fulfilled in their lusts. (He used the word 'lusts' with gusto.) In other words, he did not know *what he believed in*. Just as a person who 'believes in the stars' does not know *what they believe in*. Psalm 135:15–18 puts it perfectly.

> 15. *The idols of the nations are silver and gold, the work of men's hands.*
>
> 16. *They have mouths, but they do not speak; Eyes they have, but they do not see;*

17. They have ears but they do not hear; Nor is there any breath in their mouths.

18. Those who make them are like them; So is everyone who trusts in them.

So we can see that the 'image' of the idolater is indeed 'imagery', and that they seek to live out their lives in the strengths of their own idolatrous concepts and are limited by these insecure concepts and imaginations. They have replaced the reality of God as the source of their lives and hoped in a phantom.

When I say that they have 'replaced' God, that is what I really mean, because God has placed within man the ability to believe in Him. God has placed the evidence of His reality in His own creation, and if man were humble enough to admit it, he would fall on his knees and give God glory for who He is. That is why this is the *first* commandment, as upon this rests the basis of everything that means reality to us.

20. For since the creation of the world His invisible attributes are clearly seen, being understood by the things that are made, even His eternal power and Godhead, so that they are without excuse,

21. because, although they knew God, they did not glorify Him as God, nor were thankful, but became futile in their thoughts, and their foolish hearts were darkened.

22. Professing to be wise, they became fools,

23. and changed the glory of the incorruptible God into an image made like corruptible man – and birds and four-footed beasts and creeping things.

24. Therefore God has also given them up to uncleanness, in the lusts of their hearts, to dishonour their bodies among themselves,

25. who exchanged the truth of God for the lie, and worshipped and served the creature rather than the Creator, who is blessed forever. Amen.

Romans 1:20–25

2. Religious Idolatry

This is very similar to Cult idolatry, except that it is more specialised, in that it seeks to deal with the orthodoxy of God

Himself, and to limit Him with our own religious or traditional concepts. This is what Israel did in the account mentioned previously with the golden calf.

The disciple Peter also fell in this way by enshrining the Jewish religious traditions when he was told to take the gospel of grace to the Gentiles (Acts 10:9–16). He said 'No' to God when he was told to 'take up and eat' of the four footed creatures that were lowered in the sheet whilst he was in a trance on his rooftop, praying. Religious tradition is the only power that can get man to say 'No' to God and still feel quite righteous and holy about it! 'Christian' religious tradition often fails in much the same way.

Identity and Fatherhood

Our identity as children in the family of God comes through God's fatherhood in our lives. It is a documented fact and a counselling truism that delinquent behaviour patterns and subsequent emotional disorders, particularly those related to identity crises and indications of a low appreciation of self-worth, involve some kind of breakdown in the father–child relationship.

This does not always reflect an uncaring father role in the situations where a poor father–child relationship has occurred, as other factors may be involved that affect the maintenance of the relationship. These can be such things as illness, or separation forced by circumstances beyond normal control, and including of course, even premature death of a father. But the fact is that our ultimate self-identity which comes from the quality of our relationship with our Father God, has a flow-on effect through to the role of earthly fatherhood.

The evidence is convincing, if not conclusive, that not only sons derive a sense of their 'maleness' from their fathers, but that daughters also, derive a sense of their 'femaleness' from their relationship with their fathers. In fact the current sociological phenomenon of the women's liberation movement, is a direct result of the poor treatment that women have received from men. The bitterness and resentment felt by so many women toward men is a result of their not being protected by them, as the order of God ordained it to be.

A daughter, loved and protected by her father will feel comfortable and at ease in being a woman and perceive herself to be in a man's *and* a woman's world, and so not try to take upon herself a man's role responsibilities in order to feel secure, or identified as a 'person'. Her expectations and values regarding men and their role as provider and protector will also be in perspective in guiding her choice of a life partner, arming her with the wisdom for proper choices. This also has another flow-on effect of setting a standard for men, that if perceived by thinking males, would motivate them to be 'the right man' for 'the right woman'.

The Church and the Father

Paul places the identity of the Church squarely in the arena of its relationship with our heavenly Father, when he refers to us as being 'named' by our Father.

> 14. *For this reason I bow my knees to the Father of our Lord Jesus Christ,*
> 15. *from whom the whole family in heaven and earth is named.* Ephesians 3:14, 15

A person's name is a mark of their identity, and tells them and others *who they are*. Our name comes from our Father, through His Son Jesus Christ. That is why we are called 'Christians'. (We are also referred to as the 'Bride' of Christ.)

Now the point I am making is this. The religious idolatry that the Church has practised is due to the *identification* with a denomination or Church tradition, rather than with that of The Father. This has been the cause of such obvious division as is historically and currently seen in the Church. So instead of the unity that is available through the *One Father, we have missed that and opted for the 'name' that comes by parading our independences, and emphasising our differences. Is it any wonder that God cannot be very much glorified in the earth through His Church, when she is doing what Israel did in its hey-day of idolatry and 'high places'.*

3. Ideological Idolatry

This kind of idolatry has as its image or idol, and idea, or 'ism' that promises fulfilment, purpose, and identity to its followers. (I'm waiting for the day when all the '*is*ms' have become '*was*ms'.) The following is a very short list of 'isms' (some of which are generally regarded as being quite respectable), that currently boast of many adherents.

Communism, nationalism, humanism, patriotism, denominationalism, liberalism, capitalism, etc. We should note also that not all adherents to these ideologies are idolaters, but that they only become idolaters when they look to these ideas or ideals for their life fulfilment and identity.

Putting an 'ism' on the end of a word is not only labelling that idea or philosophy, but it is magnifying it in its ideal form. When you think of an 'ism', say communism, or capitalism, you tend not only to think of the philosophy of the basic idea, but you also picture the type of person, or more essentially, the type of group identity, that you associate with the idea. 'Isms' attract people who attract other people to the essence of the central belief system contained in the idea or ideal.

This attraction is an inspirational one, because it 'inspires', which means it gives breath, or life (the opposite of 'expires'). And some ideals are most inspiring. *But a relationship with an ideal is not the same as a relationship with a person.* And this is the problem with ideological idolatry – It is a substitute for a relationship with a person.

Remember that I said earlier that *the commandments were a function of relationships.* All true growth of character, especially concerning Godly values, comes through the agency of people–people relationships – God has designed life to be that way. His whole meaning for us is contained in the fact that He is a *person*, and not just a concept or an ideal.

Now people involved in an 'ism' will of necessity be relating to other people, but the basis of their acceptance in that relationship will not be because of who that person is in themselves, but in how they follow the 'form of worship' of the ideology they have in common. Unorthodoxy is not allowed. This is why Jesus found himself in trouble with the scribes and Pharisees of His day, because of his 'unorthodoxy', when in fact he was the most orthodox of all because he was relating to his Father as he should have, and as *they* should have. He said that the true worshippers would worship the Father in spirit and in truth, for indeed the Father was seeking *such to worship Him* (John 4:20–24).

Idolatry and Worship

The word 'worship' is an interesting word. It comes from the old English word, 'worthship', and this denotes that the object of worship is that which is most **worth**while to the worshipper. In the passage from John's gospel mentioned above, Jesus also said, '*You know not what (or who) you worship.*' In other words, the religious people of the day found a sense of worth in a form of religion rather than in a person.

Now let us look at what it means to find 'worth' in something, or in somebody. Worth is measured, not in what one *has*, but in **what one** *has to give*. God not only owns everything. *(The earth is The Lord's, and all its fullness.* Psalm 24:1), but He gives of all He has, to man. He alone is 'worthy'.

Therefore our worth is not measured in what we have of ourselves. We really have nothing of ourselves. What we have, we have only because it was given by God. But what we have been given by God, through Jesus Christ is of enormous worth, if it could only be perceived for its true value. As Paul states,

> '*the eyes of your understanding being enlightened; that you may know what is the hope of His calling, what are the riches of the glory of His inheritance in the saints*'.
>
> Ephesians 1:18

Our worship of God is our statement of acknowledgment that God is worth everything to us, in that He owns us and gives us our sense of worth. *Therefore* by substituting some ideology for the person of God, we are devaluing ourselves as His creatures, and seeking to find worth and meaning in something that can only give us what we put into it. Ideological idolatry is an enormously costly exercise to the human soul. It demands total commitment and offers only its own name in return.

4. Hero Worship

In this form of idolatry, self identity is sought through identifying with the achievements, charisma and status of others such as sports champions, entertainers (rock **idols**), politicians and statesmen, and religious leaders. This kind of behaviour, called 'emulation' in the scriptures, is condemned, along with witchcraft, and even idolatry itself, as one of the works of the flesh (Galatians 5:20).

Here again, as in ideological idolatry, there is a fine line between admiring something and taking that thing to oneself, or life fulfilment and identity. Role-modelling has a very legitimate function in helping to set standards and an example to follow. Paul the apostle gave his own life and pattern of behaviour as a model to follow in the faith, and he told us to be followers of him as he was of Christ. Paul would have been aghast at any attempts by other Christians to dress like him or follow his manner of speech inflection, or personality traits. He did not want clones of himself, but rather wanted to see all men conformed to the image of Christ. He also held up Church leaders (thereby setting them a great challenge), when he told the church to follow their faith and to watch their manner of life (Hebrews 13:7).

It is possibly because role-modelling is not demonstrated in today's society and in the Church the way it should be, that we have the exploitation of peoples' lives, and especially young people, to the point that they form entire subcultures around the heroes that are held up to them. These are endorsed by advertising companies, the media and the clothing and fashion industry. The 'hero' himself, or herself, may not be at fault in promoting this image identity, but there is no doubt that the place of adulation that the hero is given, is a temptation to pride and self-glory.

This is where it is important for a person to know the difference between 'receiving honour' and 'taking glory'. God wants us to honour one another as members of His body, and as children in His family. That is, to give one another place and recognition for gifts and enablings. This is for the purpose of serving one another and *giving to one another, out of what He has given to us.* Then true *worth* is being expressed and understood, as being not only that which we have, **but that which we have, to give.**

5. Self-Image Building

This is the most widespread form of idolatry, and in fact, all the other forms of idolatry can be seen to be expressions of this basic attitude of insecurity. A secure person will know *who* they are and *why* they are, and will know where they came from and also where they are going, not in the sense that they can predict their own future, but they can entrust their future into God's hands, being assured that God, as their Father, is personally committed to their life fulfilment as objects of His love and purpose for them, just as would be the sentiments of any loving and caring father for his own children.

Jesus made a statement of *where* He came from and *what* His purpose was, when He said in the gospel of John (6:38), *'For I have come down from heaven, not to do My own will, but the will of Him who sent Me.'* Jesus knew who he was, where he was going, and why he was going there. He did not have to build for himself an image or a reputation, and in fact, made himself of *no* reputation, that he might fulfil His reason for existence more perfectly. When we understand that our lives are 'hid in Christ' we are content to be 'found in Him' and not in some fruitless search for 'self discovery' that exhausts our soul.

Self-image building usually involves two steps. The first is *self rejection* and the second is *self projection*. We will deal with self rejection first.

Self Rejection

Since all self-image building is to establish for *ourselves* a sense of identity, apart from that found in our Father God, through Jesus Christ, it must be false, and must also involve *rejection* of our true selves. Self rejection most often begins as a result of a parental lack in providing the attention and loving discipline so needed by children.

Being given attention provides the focus of being 'special', and an object of value and worth. Demands for attention are normal in a child because each child gets to know its boundaries in this way. Behaviour that is suitable and pleasing gets approval, and behaviour that is unsuitable gets disapproval. If this is communicated in a loving way, without *rejection*, then it is a form of training which allows the child to understand its boundaries concerning acceptable behaviour. There is no such 'instinct' for such understanding, and it must be learned. The only means for such learning is from the responses of the parent. That is why attention and discipline go hand in hand. A child can always feel 'special' because indeed they are special, just as we are special to God, as the 'apple of His eye'.

Lack of attention and the subsequent lack of disciplinary adjustment and correction of confused ideas as to what is acceptable behaviour, is then usually reinforced by external pressures. These often take the form of peer group pressures and a conformity to some kind of subculture, where acceptability and attention can be won by going along with the crowd, and so sacrificing the integrity of one's own real worth and identity.

Quite often the self rejection involved in such experiences does not always appear as inferiority, but is almost as often seen as self assertiveness as a form of rebellion and pride and as a protest to the perceived rejection felt at home. The simple and perfect remedy is a revelation of *'being accepted in The Beloved'* (Eph. 1:6).

Self Projection

Self projection is the act of compensation for self rejection. It always follows self rejection, and looms 'larger than life' in attitudes of self expression. Self projection itself usually takes one or the other of two forms. These are (a) The positive or assertive type of self projection, and (b) The negative or critical type of self projection.

Type (a), The positive or assertive type of self projection follows the 'Saul' type of personality, which is a 'head and shoulders above others' kind of attitude. Saul was a man who was infatuated by his own stature, which happened to be tall, but the same attitude can be found in a person of small stature as well, such as Zaccheus, the tax collector.

Saul sought to project and to maintain his stature. He jealously fought for and guarded himself against the emerging identity of David, who was content to be the person he was in God's eyes. (Indeed, he saw himself as 'the apple of God's eye'.) Saul postured desperately in displays of bravado and domination, fearful of the disapproval of the people. When rebuked by the prophet Samuel for disobedience to God in offering a sacrifice after the battle against the Amalekites, he admitted that he feared the people, then pleaded with Samuel to honour him before the elders. If only Saul could have accepted himself as he was, and accept the boundaries of approval set by God!

Zaccheus was a man of small stature, who had tried to add to his stature by accumulating wealth through taking advantage of people as a tax collector. His story is different to Saul's in that he found a place of repentance, after having an encounter with Jesus. Being small and being the type of person that he was, he was used to taking any advantage that he could in life. Hearing that Jesus was approaching, he climbed a sycamore tree. (There were probably many 'sycamore trees' in Zaccheus' emotional life, which he scaled to try to be head and shoulders above the crowd!) However, when Jesus saw him up the tree, He said to him *come down*. Jesus wanted Zaccheus to see himself as he really was, and to know that that was the only way that he could truly come before Him.

Zaccheus received a revelation of acceptance that day, and his story has been immortalised in the scriptures, as a testimony to the grace of God. In that day, a 'taker' became a 'giver', because he discovered his true worth. He realised that he had something to give, and he was willing to give it.

When we are tempted to project ourselves in a false representation of our own identity, Jesus says to us, *come down* so that we can be who we really are before Him. None of us need be ashamed of our physical stature, or appearance, or any other attributes given to us in this life by God, for each of us has a worth and a self-reality that can find expression to the glory of God.

Some people may feel that their worth or stature can be increased by having a better position in life, by way of a prestigious job or status of some kind, and those people's lives are an endless pursuit for this kind of image. Jesus took the most lowly of tasks one day, when He washed the disciples' feet. Now foot washing also has become immortalised, and reverenced as a worthy form of ceremony. But this is because of who did it, not because of what it was in itself. In the same way, our job, no matter what it is (as long as it is honest), is worthy. In other words *our job does not give us worth, but we give it worth*, and give thanks to God.

Type (b), the negative or critical type of projection, is one who, in contrast to the type (a) who seeks to go beyond himself, actually seeks to hide within himself. This person is judgemental and critical, sometimes distant and aloof, and in some cases probing and nosy. The posture though, is one of standing in judgement, which is actually a defence against being judged, and more significantly, a defence against having to change!

Michal, David's wife, was one of these people. She despised her husband as he danced before The Lord, and her judgement was barrenness. God's judgement upon her seems harsh, but was nonetheless appropriate because her attitude stifled life and joy and the Godly self expression of her husband, David.

There are many such instances of this attitude in the scriptures, and the underlying factor in all of them is unbelief. Israel showed this attitude when they were told to go in to the promised land, and ten of the spies brought back a report that there were giants in the land and that Israel were as grasshoppers before them. The Lord punished them for this attitude of unbelief, in not seeing themselves as He saw them. Theirs was a sin again against the second commandment in taking upon themselves an image that God had not given them.

Gideon was a man who started out in unbelief, unable to grasp the reality of who he was in God's sight. God told him that he was a mighty man of valour, which was God's purpose for him, but Gideon had actually been in hiding, afraid of the Midianite army. His pitiful response to God, when challenged to become a deliverer of his people, was 'O, *my Lord, how can I save Israel? Indeed my clan is the weakest in Manasseh, and I am the least in my father's house'.* This was his perception of himself, which although factual concerning the circumstances of his birth, was irrelevant with regard to the image that God had of him.

Fortunately Gideon believed God and rose to be the man he was destined to be in God's plan for His life. The key revelation is in seeing God and not self, and thereby not frustrating the grace of God. Paul was able to say *'I am what I am by the grace of God'.* (1 Corinthians 15:10) and also to quote the word of The Lord to him that said *'My grace is sufficient for you, for My strength is made perfect in weakness'* (2 Corinthians 12:9).

Remedy and Release

The text of the second commandment, as found in Exodus ch. 20, and as written at the beginning of this chapter, includes the words *'For I, The Lord your God, am a jealous God ...'* This attribute of God's character, jealousy, is a remarkable sentiment that He has towards us, and is His remedy for our idolatry. Godly jealousy, unlike worldly jealousy, so desires the best for the object of its love, that it cannot tolerate that anything less be desired or accepted by the object of that love.

That is why God is committed to destroying idols in our lives. It is a measure of His profound love for us, that He will not let us be distracted by that which is inferior to His best for us. If we can believe this, we can be released into a rest of faith, that allows us to accept ourselves in His grace, and trust Him for the success in being who we are.

Chapter 4
Seeking of Endorsement

The Third Commandment

You shall not take the name of The Lord your God in vain, for the Lord will not hold him guiltless who takes His name in vain.

Exodus 20:7

Responsibility

This commandment commands a responsible attitude towards the name of God. This responsibility is required because of the great authority vested in the name of God.

This responsibility and this authority may be abused in the two following ways:

1. Carelessness in the testimony of our lives
As Christians we bear the name of Jesus Christ. Therefore our behaviour and speech should honour Him who is our head. Disobedience in this aspect of the commandment therefore involves:

– The vulgar use of The Lord's name (commonly called blasphemy).

– Behaviour that brings reproach upon God or His people. Paul admonished the Roman Christians for this in Romans 2:23, 24.

2. Seeking to use God's name to increase our own stature
This attitude is at the heart of God's command concerning the proper respect due His name, and will be given the greater

attention in this chapter. This is an attitude motivated by the desire to obtain God's endorsement for our own name. And this endorsement for our own name is *really the seeking of endorsement for the self images that we have been building, according to the fault addressed in the previous commandment.*

We saw in the previous chapter, which dealt with the second commandment, that man seeks to find for himself an identity, and builds images, notably *self images* that seek to express his idea of who he is. Because of the basic insecurity within every image-maker that does not fully trust in God, there is the added compulsion to attach credibility to that image by borrowing the fame or success of someone else's achievement or reputation. This is in the spirit of 'name dropping' and is common amongst the insecure and the ambitious.

This seeking of endorsement can operate at many levels, depending upon what worth or value a person attaches to the one he borrows his endorsement from. If that person happens to be a religiously motivated person, the one whose name is used is God.

The self effort required in this process of securing endorsement produces much stress and preoccupation in the life, and is manifested in one major form, which is *presumption.*

The Presumer

Presumption can look very much like faith, and deceives many people, both those who practice it and those who look on. But in fact presumption is anti-faith. It is a form of self-confidence based upon a deception.

The deception is that God isn't looking! Or to put it another way, God doesn't care, and is therefore unaware of what the presumer is doing. In the mind of the presumer God really doesn't care because He is busy doing His thing, independently, and so obliviously unaware of what other lesser beings are doing. The presumer will admit to himself however, that God may intervene in certain magic moments, especially if the presumer puts pressure on Him, as if God acted by whim – but that is up to Him.

This is the classic attitude of the idolater, and is evidenced by the strange, occultist behaviour of many idol worshippers, and their irrational incantations and repetitious calling upon the names of their gods. One example in scripture is that of the contest between Elijah and the prophets of Baal on Mt. Carmel. In this contest, Elijah was acting in faith, and the Baal worshippers were acting in presumption. Both parties expected to achieve a supernatural result, the calling down of fire from Heaven to light the sacrifice of a bull upon the altar. Elijah also expected to see God release an outpouring of rain to break the three and a half year drought.

Elijah's faith was based upon his knowledge of God and the word of The Lord that had come to him in prayer. He was not interested in his own reputation, but rather he was interested in God's name, that God would get the glory. He said to the prophets, *'Then you call on the name of your gods, and I will call upon the name of The Lord; and the God who answers by fire, He is God.'* (1 Kings 18:24) Elijah was familiar with the attitude and methods of the idolaters, and knew what was going through their minds, as presumers. He watched as they danced about, gashing themselves with knives, calling ceaselessly upon Baal from morning till noon. And so he mocked them when he said, *'Cry aloud, for he is a god; either he is meditating, or he is busy, or he is on a journey, or perhaps he is sleeping and must be awakened.'* (1 Kings 18:27) But there was no voice, and the prophets of Baal became very exhausted, as most presumers do. The result, of course, was that God answered Elijah by fire, lit the sacrifice, and then sent the rain, as was His pre-ordained purpose, which He had communicated to Elijah in prayer (James 4:17, 18).

The underlying deception of mind of the presumer is one regarding the *relational* nature of God, and His *immanence*, or ever-presence with us. He is closer to us than our own thoughts! God is not only omnipresent, He is *immanent*, that is, He is personally present *with* us. If that fact were believed by the man in the street, it would be the most startlingly life changing fact of a person's existence. It would be the biggest news of the day! The problem is that people just don't believe it, and they live like God was asleep (until they shout at Him).

Remember, all the commandments deal with relationships,

and this commandment focuses on a very real aspect of a relationship, and a very important aspect, which is, the *name* of the Person to whom we are related. It is bad enough to have one's name forgotten, but even worse, to have it abused or exploited. But with the presumer, God is perceived as being arbitrary, and non-relational, even though He is deemed to exist. That is the reason for the confusion felt, and even imparted by presumers. The whole scheme of cause and effect is misunderstood, when it comes to personal responses, and the reasons why loving people want to do things for each other, caringly and consistently.

This lack of understanding is equivalent to what I term 'spiritual autism'. Autism is a tragic condition found in certain people, who are unable to relate at a normal level. These people are typified by certain lacks in their cognisance, which include, *the inability to understand a belief system, based upon a trust relationship, the inability to respond with gratitude, and the inability to understand cause and effect concerning why things happen to them and for them through other people.*

I want to tell you of a true account of a little autistic boy, as told by his family. Little Charles was very scarce with words, and in fact hardly spoke at all. So his father taught him to point at a certain cupboard in the kitchen when he wanted some sweets and lollies. When Charles did this, his father would give him a lolly or two. Now a normal pattern in Charles' life was that he would get depressed from time to time, but there began to occur bouts of depression of more severity and of longer duration than normal. This became an obvious concern for the parents, and so his mother began to observe him more closely than ever, without Charles being aware of her doing it, and she followed him on his little wanderings about the house. It was with great sadness that she saw him one morning, standing in the kitchen, alone and unaware of her presence, pointing to the cupboard where the lollies were kept. He could not understand why no lollies were forthcoming!

This inability to understand relational cause and effect is typical of the religious presumer. He uses God's name as though he were pointing at a cupboard and expecting his desires to materialise. But just as love and grace can penetrate the world of the autistic child (and I've seen it happen), so too can God penetrate the life of the presumer. A person who fell into deep sin and suffered great shame and reproach recently, said to me that God had radically penetrated his consciousness. For four days, the man felt the severe disapproval of God upon him because of his sin, but mainly because of his presumption. He knew he could be forgiven for his sin, but he also knew that God's wrath was upon the self confidence that had become a mark of his life. This drove him to the foot of the cross, where, in his humiliation (at God's hands), he found repentance and tasted the love and mercy of his Saviour.

Presumption and despair are closely allied as destroyers of faith, because they are both based upon a false hope. If we do not have a correct hope, then we cannot have a correct faith. This is because *'faith is the substance of things hoped for'* (Hebrews 11:1). If the hope is misplaced, and based upon expectations that are presumptuous and self seeking, then God cannot meet those hopes with His faith (because all faith comes from God – Hebrews 12:2). By the same token, if there is no hope, because of despair, then there is no expectation in the relationship of God's care and provision, and even when provision is given, it is not perceived as being from a loving God. The paradox is that if a presumer does not allow the humbling hand of God upon his life to change his heart, he will end up in despair! He will not believe God for anything. This was the case with Saul, who ended up going to a witch to get direction for his life as he could not hear God any more, and this because he persisted in his desperate search for endorsement and self glory.

Have you ever heard one of those testimonies of some great act of God's provision, or miracle working power in someone's life? It inspires faith and glorifies God. But have you ever thought to yourself, 'Why doesn't that sort of thing happen to me?' But perhaps it has happened in your life and you too, can testify of the marvellous provision of God. I can think of my own experience, and be blessed by the encouragement that my testimony has meant to others.

But what if some presumptuous person, in order to seek prominence, gives a great swelling testimony of what God has done, when in fact, that person's imagination has been working overtime? That testimony has used God's name as a doorway to gain acceptance and favour, and this too, is a sin against the third commandment and will be dealt with by God.

The Faith Epistle of James

The epistle of James is an epistle written against the practice of presumption, and blasphemy, and so is an appropriate passage of scripture to include in a study on the third commandment. In fact Chapter two and verse seven says, '*do they not blaspheme the noble name by which you are called?*', referring to those who trust in riches, and oppress God's people. This epistle also mentions the faith prayer of Elijah on Mt. Carmel, in his contest with the prophets of Baal.

James speaks about a real faith, that is, a faith that works, because it comes out of relationship with God, and is not mere words, or empty believing. It might seem at first to run counter to the glorious epistle of Paul to the Romans when he espoused righteousness by faith alone, through grace, so that no man can boast of his own works. In fact, Martin Luther, whose spirit was born into liberty through the Roman epistle, had great difficulty with James' epistle, and called it 'an epistle of straw'. The difficulty was not there, in reality, and was only an apparent one, because of the particular emphases being drawn in the different letters.

But James is speaking of a real, living faith, a faith which has trials, and which requires patience, in order for it to have its perfect work. These trials, and this patience are required because a sovereign Person is involved with a sovereign will, a Person that becomes involved on a relationship level with us in our faith and requires that we work along with Him in the active expression of our faith. Presumption requires no trials and no patience – it is just words – and requires no action (at least in cooperation with God). Presumption claims all kinds of things but produces no *fruit* – (another key word in James' epistle).

The Wrong Image

The first chapter describes the double minded man who is unstable in all his ways. He is the insecure person who has fashioned an image for himself of who he is, and wavers between trusting that image that he has made (and can see), and trusting the person of God (whom he cannot see). This man is warned by James about being drawn away by his own desires and enticed, the fruit of which is sin. Also in this first chapter he exhorts us to be doers of the word, and not hearers only. *Then comes the statement concerning our self identity!* James says that the hearer, who is not a doer is like the man who sees himself in a mirror, observes himself, and goes away, *immediately forgetting what kind of man he is!* He doesn't know who he is looking at.

This is because he has confused his false sense of identity with the true identity that he is to possess in Christ. He keeps getting confused with the image of himself, that he has made, and the image into which The Holy Spirit is seeking to conform him.

The second chapter continues addressing the matter of having wrong values because of a wrong image of self, and condemns the partiality, or preference that is given to a rich man against a poor man. This is in the spirit of gaining endorsement or approval through the success or achievements of other people.

There seems to be a strange fascination by Christians with the conversion of a rich or famous person, be he, or she, a sportsman, politician, or entertainer etc. And while it can further the gospel of Jesus Christ because of greater access to people's ears if a famous person can witness to saving grace, the fact remains that *God needs no endorsement*. God does not need to have a mere mortal's name attached to His, to make His name any more noble or acceptable. The motivation of the Christian who embraces this anomaly is one of insecurity, driven by a desire to have other people give acceptability to himself and his persuasion, rather than have other people blessed by God. How much 'evangelism' is really proselytism, which is the changing of another person's persuasion to one's own persuasion, so that they too, belong to 'the club' and therefore lend more strength and credibility to the decision that you made to join 'the club'. That club can be anything you like to name, any 'ism' at all, including denominationalism. All of this is *using the Lord's name in vain*.

Words and Works

I suppose one of the main distinctions that can be observed is that presumers and proselytisers use persuasive words (and endorsements), while God uses persuasive behaviour, born of a faith that *works* through love. James uses two illustrations of real faith with real works in this chapter – Abraham and Rahab. Abraham is also the object lesson of faith in Paul's letter to the Romans, which is interesting (and significant), and both Abraham *and* Rahab appear in the 'faith chapter' of the letter to the Hebrews (Hebrews ch. 11).

Abraham demonstrated that God, and God's will were the object of his desire, rather than the promise to himself, made by God Himself, that his *seed* would be multiplied – and Isaac was his *only* seed. He was not only tested in his patience in waiting many years for Isaac, but was also tested in His trust in God, that God would spare Isaac in that fateful moment, *or raise Isaac from the dead!*. Look at this amazing testimony to faith in Hebrews 11:17–19.

> 17. *By faith Abraham, when he was tested, offered up Isaac, and he who had received the promises offered up his only begotten son,*
> 18. *of whom it was said, 'In Isaac your seed shall be called,'*
> 19. *accounting that God was able to raise him up, even from the dead, from which he also received him in a figurative sense.*

That is the kind of *real faith* that James is talking about!

And then there is the testimony of faith concerning Rahab the harlot, an ancestor of Jesus according to the genealogy in Matthew 1:5 (now *that* is a peculiar endorsement, if ever there was one!).

The story of Rahab is a strange one. It is the story of a harlot who hid some Hebrew spies when Joshua was about to take the city of Jericho. For her act of collaboration with God's people, she won fame in the faith chapter of the book of Hebrews.

But what does this have to do with *real faith* over against the problems of presumption and endorsement? Well, there are a number of significant factors involved here, which influence the weight and meaning of her decision. First, she was a harlot, and as such was of a kind typically motivated by materialism and expedience, playing for advantage and exploiting any possibility for self gain that would come her way. And secondly, what should happen, but the king of Jericho, who hears that the spies are under her roof, commands that she hand them over. What better opportunity to get favour with the most important and powerful man in the land. But her heart believed in God, and in His power of deliverance more than the king of her own people. She forsook the endorsement of a king, for faith in God, and God honoured her faith.

Christian Schizophrenia

In the third chapter James speaks of the unrestrained use of the tongue. We will deal with this more fully later when we cover the chapter on the ninth commandment which deals with bearing false witness and the illegal use of the power of the tongue. The point he strikes at here is the duplicity of those Christians who, out of the same mouth, bless God, and curse men. This is such a contradiction that it truly blasphemes God's name. He is addressing Christian Jews who are living amongst non-Christian Jews, and there would be obvious conflicts between them, but the managing of this conflict by the Christian Jews was doing nothing to further the gospel of grace that had been delivered to them.

In the fourth chapter he explains why their presumptuous prayers are not being answered. He explains that their lifestyles of conflict and self interest cause them to 'ask amiss' in their prayers and that in their pride, they are being *resisted* by God. Like all presumers, they were wanting to use God for their own ends. His simple exhortation to them was to draw near to God, and He would draw near to them.

He further admonishes them in this chapter about making plans for their own future, to go to such and such a place, stay a year, make a profit, and return. We might say, 'What's wrong with making plans?' – Nothing at all – As long as we do not make them independent from what we perceive to be in line with God's will, and for His purpose. I believe in *flexible planning* simply because God has not given me the gift of *infallibility*! And what's more, I don't know of anyone who has it. This is the kind of 'faith' based on self-confidence and arrogance as pointed out by James in the very next verse. Again, James' point is that God is very close to us, and wants us to live a life in partnership with Him.

Wealth and Independence – or Trust

In chapter five James pinpoints one of the most powerful agents of temptation and influence upon a person that will drive them into an independence and presumption about the control they think they have over their own destiny – and that is the corrupt use of wealth, especially that gained by the oppression of others. He then encourages them again in the exercise of *real faith*, by exhorting them to be patient and endure through difficult times, trusting in the mercy and compassionate nature of The Lord.

His next caution, about not swearing on anything using an oath, but rather to giving a simple 'yes' or 'no' when giving one's word on a matter, is again, precisely what is needed to be heard by one who seeks to add endorsement to his word. Swearing by an oath is to add a name greater than your own to your promise and so add a few cubits to your own stature.

His final appeal is for that of a simple exercise of faith in our prayers to God, trusting Him for the results. He uses the simple example of prayer for the sick, by the calling of the elders of the church, and the anointing with oil, and says that *'the prayer of faith'* will heal the sick. Here, again he is talking about *real* faith, not presumption. The illustration of Elijah, as being a man of like passions as we are, is also designed to persuade us that faith is not complicated, or magic, but exercised through relationship with a divine person, who hears us and grants us the faith that brings forth the works that are pleasing in His sight.

What's in a Name?

As we have seen, a name means more than just a label or even a description. When a name gets into the public arena it becomes a reputation, and a reputation becomes its own form of identity. A reputation not only presents an *image* but it represents a *public image*, and this creates its own world of expectations, both by the public, *of* the person with the reputation and by the person *with* the reputation. A reputation becomes an extremely demanding *god* to serve. *Jesus made Himself of no reputation*. He humbled Himself, and in doing so God highly exalted Him, giving Him a '*name above every name that is named*'.

We are exhorted to have this same mind in *us*. In other words, we should not seek for honour or reputation, but for opportunities to serve, and if God wishes to endorse our service with His name, then we need to pray for the grace to manage it, and remain humbled, as Jesus did. How many ministries become shipwrecked, sailing in these treacherous waters? But on the other hand, how many men and women have graced the name of God because their own names have been a window into His goodness.

Chapter 5

Entering into Rest

The Fourth Commandment

Remember the sabbath day, to keep it holy.

Exodus 20:8

A Day or a Life

New Testament scripture reveals that this commandment refers not to a ritual observance of one day in each week, but in the life of faith, which is the *rest* that we enter into as Christians, in the finished work of Christ. This rest is spoken of in the epistle of Paul to the Hebrews.

> 9. *There remains therefore a rest for the people of God.*
> 10. *For he who has entered His rest has himself also ceased from his works as God did from His.*
> 11. *Let us therefore be diligent to enter that rest, lest anyone fall after the same example of disobedience.*

Hebrews 4:9–11

It follows then, that no one should come under bondage as a Christian, for not observing Old Testament prohibitions concerning the sabbath day. Every day should be a holy day for the Christian who lives in the revelation of the exchanged life of Christ, and no longer has to establish his own righteousness by the works of the law.

> 16. *Therefore let no one judge you in food or in drink, or regarding a festival or a new moon or sabbaths,*

17. *which are a shadow of things to come; but the sub-*
stance is of Christ. Colossians 2:16–17

Paul emphasised this point when he wrote to the Romans, in chapter fourteen, when he said that the Christians should receive one another, or accept one another, but not to argue about things that were doubtful, or contentious, and did not deal directly with the essentials of redemption.

1. *Receive one who is weak in the faith, but not to disputes*
over doubtful things.
2. *For one believes he may eat all things, but he who is*
weak eats only vegetables.
3. *Let not him who eats despise him who does not eat, and*
let not him who does not eat judge him who eats; for God
has received him.
4. *Who are you to judge another's servant? To his own*
master he stands or falls. Indeed he will be made to stand,
for God is able to make him stand.
5. *One person esteems one day above another; another*
esteems every day alike. Let each be fully convinced in his
own mind.
6. *He who observes the day, observes it to The Lord; And*
he who does not observe the day, to The Lord he does not
observe it. He who eats, eats to The Lord, for he gives God
thanks; and he who does not eat, to the Lord he does not
eat, and gives God thanks. Romans 14:1–6

He said this because he had observed that some Christians were observing traditions from Judaism, in order to be more pleasing to the Lord. Paul contended that these Christians while being 'weak' in the faith, and perhaps 'striving' in the wrong way, were nevertheless, seeking to please God, and as such, should be accepted, and not judged.

Some of these traditions included the abstaining from meat, and the observing of one special day a week. The conflict worked both ways (and still does), because not only were the 'traditionalists' being judged for striving, against faith and grace, but the 'liberated' were being judged for 'resting' and not having to add extras to their believing, which were not direct New Testament commands.

God stood in the middle and judged the hearts, whilst commanding them, through Paul, not to judge one another's hearts. The tendency is for Christians to justify their faith, or their works, rather than let Jesus justify by His works. For we are justified by faith, and, *after* having been justified, we can do the works that are pleasing to God, in obedience to Him, and not to a set of commands that we have endorsed, that will bestow self righteousness upon us.

Seal of Good Housekeeping

When Jesus corrected Martha, the sister of Lazarus, for being anxious and troubled about many things, it was because she had made the wrong choice of activity, unlike her sister Mary, who chose to sit at Jesus' feet and learn of Him. Martha was not doing anything 'wrong' in any moral sense, but had become engrossed with her housekeeping, in order to serve The Lord, the way she had perceived that He wanted to be served. She was doing what she knew how to do best – housekeeping, and ministering hospitality to her guests. This was admirable, and had been no doubt a blessing to Jesus many times in the past. *And it made her feel good, and she liked the approval.*

But this was precisely the problem. At this particular time, Jesus wanted Martha to come and hear what He had to say, for it was God's will for her as it was for her sister Mary. But Martha was locked into her 'self image' response. Martha felt secure in her role as a housekeeper and had trusted in that image for acceptance and approval. The approval had been reinforced many times by the appreciation of other people, especially Jesus, and so her image had become endorsed. This meant that Martha had to spend more and more effort in sustaining the image. These efforts became dead works, and prevented her from entering into the rest when Jesus required her to do so.

What Martha had done, was to sin against relationship. She had valued the worth of her own efforts to satisfy herself of *her own worth*, thus justifying herself, more than she had valued the time spent quietly in relationship with Jesus. The link between this commandment and the previous one can be clearly seen, when we see Martha's need, not only for approval, but also her out-of-place scolding of her sister Mary who had obediently chosen the response of faith.

The Lord of the Sabbath

The sabbath that The Lord was most interested in was the sabbath year that occurred every seven years, because that really tested the principle of the sabbath rest in the hearts of God's children. Israel never really had much trouble with the sabbath day once a week, and do not even until this very day. In fact the observance of the sabbath day has become more and more ritualised, to the letter of the law, as it is by Seventh Day Adventist Christians. I respect this honour that man gives to God, but I believe that it misses the point of the Lord's intention for our observing a sabbath rest.

In the book of Leviticus, in chapters twenty-five and twenty-six, it is commanded firstly, that Israel observe a sabbath year every seven years so the land can have rest. Then God pronounces that if the land does not get rest, Israel will go into captivity until the land has enjoyed its rest.

The attitude of heart that God is addressing here, is that of a heart that cannot trust God to bring forth His fruit in His way in His time. They were afraid that they would go without, and could not trust God, even though He gave them His word. He even commanded that a double blessing would come in the *sixth year* to encourage them!

> 20. *And if you say, 'What shall we eat in the seventh year, since we shall not sow nor gather in our produce?'*
> 21. *Then I will command My blessing on you in the sixth year, and it will bring forth produce enough for three years.*
> Leviticus 25:20–21

Enough for three years! That is not a double blessing – that is a *triple blessing*! But for all this Israel would not trust God. For four hundred and ninety years, since the reign of King Saul, they did not observe the sabbath rest of the land every seven years. Four hundred and ninety divided by seven equals seventy. And this is the space of time that God had them taken captive into Babylon.

Captivity

20. *And to those who escaped from the sword he carried away to Babylon, where they became servants to him and his sons until the reign of the kingdom of Persia,*
21. *to fulfil the word of The Lord by the mouth of Jeremiah, until the land had enjoyed her sabbaths, ... to fulfil seventy years.* 2 Chronicles 36:20–21

In the book of Daniel and chapter nine we see where Daniel read that same word from the book of Jeremiah (25:9–10), and knew that the years had been fulfilled, and that it was time for the deliverance of his people from captivity in Babylon.

But the point to be made is that God was looking for an attitude of faith from His people and He did not get it. And this was the second time. He had seen their unbelief in the wilderness, when they turned back at Kadesh Barnea, and were afraid to go into the promised land, because of the giants in the land. This is the incident referred to in the epistle to the Hebrews in chapter four, when He declares that they did not enter into their rest because of unbelief.

And now Israel has finally come into the promised land and can truly enter into rest – but they fail again through lack of trust and unbelief. They preferred to *work* for their own results, rather than *rest* and trust God for His results. Please do not think that I am singling out Israel as being in worse unbelief than we are! I see Christians also failing to enter into their rest – *with far better promises*. Human nature has not changed since Adam, but there are lessons to be learned, and this one is the lesson of a *faith relationship with God*.

Failing to enter into rest leads into captivity. This is a spiritual principle that God wants to teach His children in these days. When Christians try to achieve results in their own strength, that can only be achieved through God's strength, their efforts become fruitless, and emotional and spiritual bondage occurs, which is their 'captivity', in dead works.

Dead Works

Dead works can take different forms. Three major forms are:
1. *legalism*, 2. *worldliness*, and 3. *hypocrisy*.

1. Legalism

This is the attempt to gain righteousness before God and man by our own works, without faith. This follows on from the problem found in the last commandment, number three, which dealt with seeking endorsement for our image by attaching God's name to what we have established. The security found in self righteousness is a powerful religious force which has driven man throughout time.

The first man to be challenged by God for his self righteous motivation was Cain, who then murdered his own brother Abel. The reason given in the word of God for the murder in Cain's heart was that his works were actually *evil* and his brother's works were *righteous* (1 John 3:12). Abel's offering was of faith, and *for God*, not *for self*.

> *By faith Abel offered to God a more excellent sacrifice than Cain, through which he obtained witness that he was righteous, God testifying of his gifts; and through it he being dead still speaks.*   Hebrews 11:4

Jesus suffered a similar fate at the prompting of a self righteous and religious crowd of people. Christians have also persecuted other Christians with malice and murder in their hearts because of the same motivation.

Legalism has such an appeal because it lends respectability to man's flesh. It does away with the need to be humbled and repent, because all one has to do is obey certain man-made rules and regulations *in the name of The Lord*. This serves to establish pride in man rather than destroy it, and this human pride then assumes an authority over more humble people. Paul saw this killer disease spreading amongst the new churches that had been established through his preaching of a gospel of grace. Two such churches were the Galatian and the Colossian churches.

The two churches had different expressions of legalism, the

Galatian church having a *formalism* at its base, and the Colossian church having a *mysticism* at its base. We will first look at the Galatian error.

Formal Legalism
> 1. *O foolish Galatians! Who has bewitched you that you should not obey the truth, before whose eyes Jesus Christ was clearly portrayed amongst you as crucified?*
> 2. *This only I want to learn from you: Did you receive the Spirit by the works of the law, or by the hearing of faith?*
> 3. *Are you so foolish? Having begun in The Spirit, are you now being made perfect by the flesh?*
> 4. *Have you suffered so many things in vain – If indeed it was in vain?*
> 5. *Therefore He who supplies the Spirit to you and works miracles among you, does He do it by the works of the law, or by the hearing of faith?* Galatians 3:1–5

Paul saw the teaching of the law for righteousness as 'another gospel' and the most harmful danger to the life and witness of the gospel of Jesus Christ. In the previous chapter (ch. 2) of the epistle he gives the account of how he rebuked the apostle Peter for refusing to eat with the Gentiles when the Jewish Christians came down from Jerusalem to Antioch, thereby endorsing the legalism that those Jewish Christians were imposing upon the saints at Antioch, Paul's home church. He said to Peter, before them all – *'Why do you compel Gentiles to live as Jews?'* (Gal 2:14b), and then in verse 16: *'Knowing that a man is not justified by the works of the law but by faith in Jesus Christ, even we have believed in Jesus Christ, that we might be justified by faith in Christ and not by the works of the law; For by the works of the law shall no flesh be justified'*

But perhaps the most severe denouncement of their legalistic behaviour was made by Paul in chapter five and in verse four.

> *You have become estranged from Christ, you who attempt to be justified by law; You have fallen from grace.*
> Galatians 5:4

There is no worse indictment upon a Christian, than to be estranged from Christ. Again, we see how the commandments deal primarily with *relationships*.

Paul actually had the same problem to address when he wrote to the Hebrews (presuming that he wrote to the Hebrews). He was challenging and encouraging Jewish Christians, who were becoming insecure in the face of persecution, and were looking at two options for themselves. They were to either give up on God altogether, and remain safe from the persecutors, or to go back into formalism, and then be no threat to the persecutors.

The third option was to 'hold fast their profession of faith, for it held great recompense of reward'.

He reminded them of the first principles of the Christian faith in chapter six, and named *repentance from dead works* as the foundation of faith. He did not just say, repentance from sin, but *dead works*, which of course, includes sin, but strikes at the real problem, that of not being able to rest in the finished work of Christ.

Mystical Legalism

The Colossian church was situated on the main trade route to the east, and therefore had passing through it, all of the exotic and mystical teachings of the eastern religions. The people of Colossae were fair game for deception, and even after having been converted to Christianity by the gospel of grace, again through Paul's ministry, could not help but fall into the alluring mystical practices of the eastern religions to bolster their 'righteousness' as religious people.

Their main vulnerability to the false teaching was that of abstinence and self denial, which also appeals to the flesh, not because it aims at building pride, *but because it aims to build humility*! The sad fact is that the false humility so obtained is actually an inverted pride.

> 18. *Let no one defraud you of your reward, taking delight in false humility and worship of angels, intruding into those things which he has not seen, vainly puffed up by his fleshly mind,*

19. *and not holding fast to the Head, from whom all the body, nourished and knit together by joints and ligaments, grows with the increase which is from God.*

20. *Therefore, if you died with Christ from the basic principles of the world, why, as though living in the world, do you subject yourself to regulations –*

22. *'Do not touch, do not taste, do not handle,'*

22. *which all concern things which perish with the using – according to the commandments and doctrines of men?*

23. *These things indeed have an appearance of wisdom in self-imposed religion, false humility, and neglect of the body, but are of no value against the indulgence of the flesh.*
Colossians 2:18–23

When either of these two legalisms is active in a church, there exists a legalistic 'peer pressure' which brings condemnation to many, and a general deadness in the church. God's people should be regarded as attractive in their *joy*, not their *austerity*.

2. Worldliness

By 'worldliness' here, I am not merely talking about a slackness in Christians regarding the pursuit of ungodly pleasures in the world. That attitude is a departure from faith and a sanctified life, that evidences itself in some way in all of the commandments, because of sin and selfishness.

What I am mainly addressing is the striving for success or achievement in the things of God, by using the methods and strategies of the world, with the attitudes of the world, rather than applying the principles of God, through faith. We can have what look like Godly goals, but they are really self motivated goals aimed at achieving glory or approval, or acceptance, or recognition, rather than to please God, and serve His people.

> *For whatever is born of God overcomes the world. And this is the victory that has overcome the world – our faith.*
> 1 John 5:4

This truth has an antithesis, or an opposite, and that is, that whatever is born of the world, can overcome our faith, when we let dead works *replace* faith. Some of the worldly philosophies that can gain a foothold are: *Competitiveness, people pleasing, and authoritarianism.*

Competitiveness and people pleasing seem to go hand in hand, because the drive to win success *against* God's people, is usually to make an impression *on* God's people. Paul spoke into this problem when writing to the Corinthian Church. They were carnal, because they competed with one another in the area of giftings, reputations, and attaching themselves to men – God's men – such as Paul, Appollos and Cephas, in order to boast against one another. Paul condemned this, because he saw the division and disunity that was caused by this attitude of the flesh. The world had begun to overcome that church, until even the other kind of worldliness came through the open door, that of gross immorality, which Paul had to discipline severely. The one often leads to the other.

One final word about competitiveness. When Jesus was teaching His disciples about faith and believing in the gospel account of John chapter five, He talks about people wanting to receive honour from one another instead of from God only. He says, in verse forty four, *'How can you believe, who receive honour from one another, and do not seek the honour that comes from the only God?'* What He has actually said is, that we remain in unbelief, if we are competing with one another for honour. Could Jesus have been putting His finger on the very reason that there is so much unbelief in the Church today?

Authoritarianism is a most subtle of worldly attitudes, because it can be rationalised by determined people with the use of the scriptures. We will be covering the proper attitudes towards authority in the next chapter which deals with the fifth commandment *'Honour thy father and thy mother'*. But it needs to be said here that striving to exercise dominion over God's people in the name of 'serving' as a leader, is one of the things that God condemns. Jesus spoke clearly against this when He saw His own disciples confusing the authority of His kingdom with that of the world. They were competing for place and position in His kingdom, and He told them that the rulers of the Gentiles exercised dominion over them, but with their leadership and ministry it must not be so. That is because authoritarianism takes leadership out of the realm of grace and puts it once again into law, and ruling through fear instead of love and faith.

Jesus changed the order of things when He put His flesh to death on the cross. He established true authority and 'Kingdom success' through that act of obedience to The Father. All true service to God comes through the cross in our lives, in simply allowing our flesh with all of its strivings and insecurities and ambitions, to surrender.

A Torn Veil

'Somebody's going to pay for this, Moishe!' An angry high priest was glaring at the veil in the temple that was rent from top to bottom the day before, when that pretender had been nailed to a cross.

'Probably vandals Rabbi, or religious fanatics – there's a lot of them around at the moment.'

'Whoever it was, they'll pay for this with their life!'

How true. A life was torn apart, and Jesus' spirit left his torn body to lay in a tomb, while He secured the keys of Hell and Death as the King of Glory. The Bible says that the veil was His flesh (Hebrews 10:20), and on that day Jesus put an end to works of the flesh as being acceptable worship to God.

Can you imagine the temple that next day, as the priests and the orthodox believers went to offer sacrifice. There was no more sacrifice for sins. It was finished. There was no more righteousness by the law, but yet the law could now be fulfilled in all righteousness, because of the Spirit of life in Christ that was available through faith in Him (Rom. 8:4).

I remember the early days of my ministry. For the first two years I tried so hard for God. I had tried so hard for everybody! But I was really trying so hard for me. I was taking a couple of weeks off with the family, in a seaside town, north of where we lived, recovering from concussion caused by a knock on the head in a 'friendly' game of football between two churches. The recovery was taking longer than it should because of the fatigue and stress I had put myself through in the past two years. I was feeling pretty despondent about continuing on in ministry, and

I began to consider returning to my former profession as a pharmacist. At least I could handle that job, with less of a toll on my life.

My prayers to God for peace were getting nowhere, and anxiety was starting to set in. I looked back over the past two years at all the hard work that I had done, and could see, that while a lot of it had been effective and had blessed people, there had been an underlying motive in back of much of my labour. Part of my motivation was to get approval from God, for myself, not just to please Him. I began to see this as 'dead works' and entered into a different kind of labour – the labour to enter into His rest. But I was not sure where to begin.

Who Works for Who?

It so happened that during this time I had occasion to take my three year old son, Matthew, out to do some shopping for the family. We were in a large department store and we came to an escalator, or moving stairway, and next to it was a regular stairway. Crowds were bustling to get on the escalator and the regular stairway was quite free. My first impulse was to bound up the stairway, and not waste time waiting for a place on the escalator. But my body was just too tired, and my mind said 'wait, don't hurry, don't strive – *this time*'. Was it my mind or was it the Lord?

It must have been the Lord, because as I picked up my son and stepped onto the escalator, I remember two streams of thinking going through my head at the same time. One was that I was telling the Lord that I would step out of His way, and that if He wanted to use someone instead of me for His purposes, then that would be fine by me, and I repented of getting in His way with my dead works. I just wanted to walk with Him. The other impression of thought was of what I was physically doing at that precise moment. I was carrying my son, and I was being carried, evenly and steadily up to the next landing! I was being carried, and getting there faster than if I was doing the work, on the stairway. Then the revelation of rest came to me, and it was as though I heard The Lord speak – 'My son, I now approve of your works.' My entire being relaxed, and joy surged through my spirit, into my soul. I had entered into the rest! I kissed my son and began to laugh. People began to give funny looks to this very happy shopper.

My life changed radically from that day onwards. I rested and recovered with a new energy and vitality that came straight from the throne of grace. It was only a matter of weeks and my wife, Tineke (who believed in me more than I did), and Matthew, and Jessica, our little four year old daughter (who thought her dad was 'tops' too), and I, went to live in that very place where I had gone for the 'rest', and we pioneered our first church there. To complete the account of our family history to date, I must add, that twelve years later my wife and I had another daughter, Lucy, who is now nearly four years old (and has definitely *not* learned to rest).

The interesting fact was that even though I had entered into rest, the activity and productivity of the ministry increased, but this time without the fatigue and stress. I had learned that Jesus was more interested and blessed by my relating to Him, than by my trying to 'impress' Him with my works. It was in this relationship that I could get to know Him more, and His heart for His people, and so be more obedient to His will.

3. Hypocrisy

This, of all forms of dead works, appears to be the most futile and vain. The word in the Greek language actually means 'actor'. If you wanted to pay a compliment to a Greek actor, you would say to him or her – 'What a great hypocrite you are!' To many people, the world may indeed be a stage, as in William Shakespeare's 'Macbeth' where players strut and fret their way across. But the church is no place for actors, as far as living a real life is concerned. Walking in the light means being real, and to talk one way and to live another way brings down the final curtain very swiftly (even though it may take years).

Again, God's judgement is severe on this form of dead works, as seen in the scathing words of Jesus to the scribes and Pharisees.

> 13. *'But woe to you, scribes and Pharisees, hypocrites! For you shut up the kingdom of heaven against men; for you neither go in yourselves, nor do you allow those who are entering to go in.*

14. *'Woe to you, scribes and Pharisees, hypocrites! for you devour widows' houses, and for a pretence make long prayers. Therefore you will receive greater condemnation.* 15. *'Woe to you, scribes and Pharisees, hypocrites! for you travel land and sea to win one proselyte, and when he is won, you make him twice as much a son of hell as yourselves.'*   Matthew 23:13–15

The damaging effects of the hypocrite can be clearly seen in the above passage of scripture. Because of their influence the kingdom of Heaven is shut up against others. This is because people have a tendency to copy the behaviour of an impressive person, and to adopt his values and attitudes. Something of the spirit of the hypocrite gets imparted. A hypocrite may say the right words, but he imparts the wrong spirit. If you have measles and tell people that you have mumps, what do you think they will catch? Right, they will catch measles, because no matter what you say, that is what is really there.

Other effects of the hypocrite are seen in their taking advantage of the deprived, or widows, and their preoccupation with long empty prayers. And in the third verse, we note the great effort that a hypocrite makes to gain a convert. Even with a missionary vision to travel overseas, they stumble over their very own deception.

The flesh is afraid of its own weaknesses, and seeks to either strengthen them with self effort, or cover them with a false covering, rather than take them to the cross, where the life of Jesus can be given in exchange. Great rest comes when we learn to be ourselves, by His grace, and take His image more seriously than we do our own.

Why did God Rest?

The word of God says – in the same passage that contains the fourth commandment – that God created the world in six days, and on the seventh day He rested from His labours. Have you ever wondered why God rested? Did God have to rest? Was He weary? No, of course not. Yet He rested and commands us to rest.

Remember that I have been stating that the key thought in all the commandments is that of relationships. Now this is precisely the reason that God rested. God wanted to be *at rest* so that He could *enjoy* His creation and relate to it. Namely to relate to man, whom He had created. And this is the reason that He wants us to enter into His rest with Him, so that we can more fully do what we were created to do, and that is, to relate to Him. How cunning of the serpent to tempt man to establish his own righteousness, and eat of the tree of knowledge. And how suitable was God's judgement upon man, to cause him to 'work by the sweat of his brow, to get bread.'

Satan's plan has not changed. He does not mind how hard we work for our righteousness, and how much we sacrifice to look religious. All he does not want is that we begin to relate to The Father, through Jesus. When the disciples asked Jesus what they must do to do the works of God, Jesus answered them and said, '... *This is the work of God, that you believe in Him whom He sent.*' (John 6:29)

We have the example of Jesus to follow, and also the life of Jesus to live, just the way He described how He lived His life with His Father. He said he did *nothing* without The Father, and only that which his Father told him to do. That is why he appeals to us, to abide in the vine, so that we shall bear fruit. The fruit will not be *our* fruit only, but his fruit, because he is the vine, and we are the branches, and that is the meaning of the rest of faith.

Chapter 6

Who's the Boss?

The Fifth Commandment

Honour your father and your mother, that your days may be long upon the land which the Lord your God is giving you.   Exodus 20:12

From God to Man

The last four commandments dealt with the relationship that we have with God, and now the next six commandments deal with our relationships with one another. In order to obey the first four commandments, we need to have established quite a mature response to God. Being able to spiritually obey the 'sabbath' comes by way of experiencing some very challenging trials of faith in our walk with The Lord, whether we are talking about an Old Testament obedience (regarding the sabbath year), or a New Testament obedience, in resting in the finished work of Christ.

So while it is correct and logical, and in order, that the commandments dealing with a relationship with God come first, it is a fact in our experience, that our dealings with people, from the very day of our birth, come *before* we start consciously responding in faith and obedience to God. The first relationship we have in life is one of being under authority – with *our parents*. Other relationships with authority dealt with in this chapter are, *marriage, the Church, employment, and the State.*

Parental Authority

Our relationship with our parents is one of total dependence upon people who run our lives completely. Whether we like it or not, we start out in life by being under authority – and we would not have it any other way. We are given all we need (in normal circumstances), and are generally pretty happy and jolly about our lot, for the first few years at least. We cry a lot, get our own way a lot, probably get smacked a little – or a lot – (but we get more cuddles than smacks), and it looks for a while like we have set sail for happy days forever.

Then something goes wrong and things begin to change. A conflict becomes very distinct between parent and child. What is it? What is it that happens to spoil the perfect plot for a happy ending? Do parents all of a sudden get mean and nasty? Do they get sick and tired of all that cleaning up after us, feeding us, losing us in crowds and going frantic looking for us? Do we begin to spoil their fun? – or maybe they've got enough photographs now, and they're just bored.

It is nothing that simple unfortunately. No degree of perfection in parents is ever going to produce a child that is devoid of rebellion. The results of the fall of Adam and Eve are inherited in every child that is born of natural parents in this earth. That is why the Bible says that *'Foolishness is bound up in the heart of a child, but the rod of correction will drive it far from him'* (Proverbs 22:15). This 'foolishness' is not related to any lack of intelligence or even silly playful behaviour. It is the attitude of a hard heart – determined to have its own way. And life now becomes a series of lessons divinely designed to soften that heart, till it nestles securely and with trusting obedience in the bosom of the Father.

In the study of the last commandment we saw how the effects of independence from God in our adult life and striving in our own strength to achieve our ambitions, led to frustration and fruitlessness in our efforts. This frustration also brought fatigue and bondage into the life. This commandment, which relates to earthly authority, in the form of parental authority (even though we will cover earthly authority in general under this commandment), is to be seen as God's way of providing a framework that will teach us to relate properly and wisely to *all* authority. In this way we can be set free from the anxiety born out of independent self-effort. God wants us to be trained to receive the covering and security that comes from the care of a loving authority towards us.

It's Impossible Dad!

Let me tell you a story of a father with three sons. The father owned some land that needed some trees cleared on it, to prepare it for sowing. So he asked the first son if he would take the axe and begin chopping down some trees. There was just under half an acre to be cleared, which is quite a large area to be worked by hand, and the trees were called 'ironbark' because of their hardness. It was a very hot day.

The first son went out obediently to do the work for his father, and took the axe from the shed. He found that the axe was quite blunt on its edge and the handle was badly secured at its base. Nevertheless, he began to wield the axe. He started to sweat heavily in the hot sun, and, to make matters worse, the head of the axe kept falling off the handle, and he was not making much impression on the hard wood with the blunt edge as well. His mind began to think of the cool waters of the river that ran through the property, not far away from where he was working. The more he thought about the river, the more he thought that his father must have made a mistake, and wasn't aware of the hardness of the trees, the heat of the day, and the terrible state of repair of the axe. He knew that the sensible thing to do was to forget the clearing, and go for a swim. Dad wouldn't mind. But Dad, who was doing some paper work in his office, saw through the window what his son had decided, and was disappointed.

So the father asked his second son to do the work with the axe, which had been put back in the shed. The second son went out obediently to do what his father had told him to do. When the second son started into the job, he found he was having the same difficulties that his brother had been having. The axe was blunt, the head kept flying off the handle, and was it hot! But this boy was made of sterner stuff. Dad said 'do it' so he would do it. Nothing was going to conquer him. He had shown everyone plenty of times how determined and strong willed he was – This was just another challenge, even though Dad was a bit 'stupid' to think that any ordinary person would stand a chance of finishing the job, given the circumstances. He kept at it until almost midday when the axe head flew off once too many times and bounced off the tree onto his foot, bruising it badly. He retired hurt, and hobbled off, much to his frustration. Dad saw through the window what had happened, and was disappointed.

So the father asked the third son to do the work with the axe, which had been left lying in the field. The third son went out obediently to do what his father had told him to do. When the third son started into the job, he found he was having the same difficulties that his two brothers had been having.

The third son also found the axe too blunt, the axe head kept flying off the handle, and boy, was it hot! He kept at it though, for almost an hour when he paused and began to think to himself.

'My dad is not stupid', he thought to himself. 'He must know what's going on. He is wise enough to know that this job cannot be done under these conditions, so I'll go and have a talk to him about it – there's sure to be an answer.'

He picked up the axe and began walking towards the house. His father saw him coming, and hope was raised in his heart. The third son came into his father's office, sat down, and said,

'Dad, it's impossible!'

'What is my son?'

'The axe is too blunt, and the head keeps flying off, and it's just so hot out there, I've tried to do what you said to, but it's just not working, so I thought I'd come and talk to you about it.'

Joy swept over his father's face. This was what his father wanted, not neglect, or self determined frustration, but trust.

'Of course. Let me help, first we'll sharpen that axe, and then I'll put a wedge in at the top, to hold the head on, and how about if I come down and have a swing myself!'

There is a scripture in Ecclesiastes that sums up the story.

> *If the axe is dull, and one does not sharpen the edge, then he must use more strength; but wisdom brings success.*
>
> Ecc 10:10

As our Father, God does want us to have success, but not by our determined efforts. He wants us to work *with* Him, not just *for* Him, and He does not want us to give up in despair. Rather He wants us to trust Him and submit to His wisdom in the circumstances of our life. He wants us to recognise that His authority is not a harsh driving one, but a gentle leading one, by His Spirit, that brings us into sonship and *partnership* with Him (Romans 8:14).

The Role of Authority

The role of authority is to provide the *direction, correction, and instruction*, needed to cause us to grow in wisdom and stature and favour with God and man, that God has destined for each of His children. The scriptures show us that this was the way that Jesus grew (Luke 2:51–2), in subjection to his earthly parents, the foundation being set for a productive and fulfilling life.

1. Direction
Every life needs direction and purpose. Direction can ideally be set by one in authority, because that person has had experience enough to know the end from the beginning in many matters relating to specific life issues. This means that the one in authority can advise about the consequences of certain actions, giving the cautions and encouragements that are necessary. This comes to us from God both through the principles found in His word and through the leading of the Spirit, spoken of before in Romans 8:14.

> *For as many as are led by the Spirit of God, these are the sons of God.*
>
> Romans 8:14

2. Correction
An account of the story of Eli the priest appears in the first book of Samuel, from chapters one to four. Eli had two sons,

Phinehas and Hophni. They were disobedient sons who brought shame on their father because of their disgraceful behaviour with the women who came to the tabernacle of God. When Eli heard about these things, he complained to his sons, and said, 'why do you do such things?' He warned them of God's judgement, but giving verbal warnings was as far as his discipline and correction went! And his sons did not heed him.

God sent a messenger to speak to Eli, to remind him of his responsibility as a father and as a priest, and condemned him for not restraining his sons, and accused him of honouring his sons more than God. He pronounced judgement upon the two sons, which came to pass when they were killed in battle against the Philistines. Eli fell and broke his neck and died when he heard of the death of his sons, completing the judgement upon the lack of correction of his children.

Unfortunately the attitude of Eli is a typical one amongst many parents, who think it is sufficient to merely 'talk' to children, to get them to behave. The 'talking' often becomes shouting, but this is no more effective as a correction, it is just louder 'talking'. Unless correction is accompanied by appropriate action and restraints, when required, then the heart of the child becomes convinced that he is in control of the situation and will never experience the restraints that will drive 'foolishness' out of his heart.

> *Because the sentence against an evil work is not executed speedily, therefore the heart of the sons of men is fully set in them to do evil.*   Ecclesiastes 8:11

It is one thing to give direction, but is another thing to keep that life on course after the direction has been set. The parent who does not discipline and chastise his child is said in the scriptures not to love that child.

> *He who spares his rod hates his son, but he who loves him disciplines him promptly.*   Proverbs 13:24

Many parents fear to lose their children's love or approval if they use proper measures of discipline, and they think that they are being loving by refraining from such discipline. The opposite is true.

There is a Godly balance to be exercised in all discipline, that allows the discipline to be an act of faith, and not an act of reaction or retaliation. Proper correction is meant to strengthen the relationship, not to weaken it, and the care and the credibility of the authority must be established in each encounter by loving consistent action. I believe that a parent should stay close to a child in a time of correction, and not always send them off to their room for punishment. God stays close to us when He deals with us, even though at times His presence may seem awesome. The act of restraint need not always be a physical 'rod' either, as the Hebrew word for 'rod' is the same as that used for 'sceptre' which was the symbol of authority used by Kings. The main thing is that authority is exercised, and action is taken that brings corrective restraint to rebellious behaviour.

The Other Side

In the sixth chapter of the epistle of Paul to the Ephesians, he begins by addressing children on this very commandment. His directive is to the children first, to obey the first verse of the chapter, and then he 'targets' the fathers. He charges the fathers *'do not provoke your children to wrath, but bring them up in the training (nurture) and admonition of The Lord'*.

The provoking of children to wrath is the taking of unfair advantage of the lesser physical strength or status of the child, and asserting one's superiority in an unjust way. This 'pulling of rank' robs the child of dignity at that point, and incites a frustration and anger which is either left suppressed in the child, or expressed destructively in some other way. The child provoked in such a way often pays dearly for this experience as resistance is made against other forms of authority, and the child grows up with a general mistrust of all authority.

In that same verse, we saw that the child is to be brought up in the training (nurture) and admonition of The Lord. The word 'training' or 'nurture' is from the Greek word 'paediea' and involves the active elements of disciplinary correction that we have been discussing under the heading of 'correction.' The other word used in this verse relating to the bringing up of children is 'admonition' from the Greek, *noutheteo*, which means 'to put in mind', or to instruct.

3. Instruction

There is little point in directing or correcting a child, or an adult for that matter, without bringing instruction as well. Part of the 'forming' of a life is the 'informing' of a life. This means that teaching is included in the training of a child, so that he understands the correct values, *and* attitudes, that equip him for staying on course.

> *Train up a child in the way he should go, and when he is old he will not depart from it.* Proverbs 22:6

While ever we live, we should learn, and as we learn we should teach. Paul admonished the Hebrew Christians in Chapter five of the epistle to the Hebrews, when he said:

> 'For though by this time you ought to be teachers, you need someone to teach you again the first principles of the oracles of God; and you have come to need milk and not solid food.' Hebrews 5:12

We can only learn from someone who knows better than we do, and so we are *always* putting ourselves under that kind of schooling, and therefore recognising the authority of a teacher. Jesus was the greatest teacher that ever lived, and has left us The Holy Spirit and His word to instruct us in the truths and values of life. He taught as one with *authority*, and not as the scribes (Matthew 7:29), but what did this mean, to teach with *authority*? – It means that what he *said*, people *did*! – People did what Jesus said, because He taught clearly, so that there was understanding, and He showed people *how* to do what He said, through example and illustration. Teaching anyone is a great privilege and calling, but with it goes the responsibility and accountability of teaching what is *right* (James 3:1).

Getting it Right

The way to know that what we teach is right, is to teach the principles of life contained in the Word of God. There has been a 'move of God' in recent years, from about the mid to late 1970s where Christian schools have been raised up, offering Christ-centred education. Hundreds of thousands of children from Christian homes (mostly) are being *trained up in the way they should go*. This Christ-centred education is preparing a generation for Godly leadership in a society that has discarded absolute values for humanism and its relative values. This movement is growing in numbers and in influence all across the world.

One simple way for parents to start a Bible instruction program for their children, is to read to them from the book of Proverbs. I have followed this practice myself, and have advised many other parents to do so. The instruction and insights that are available in this wonderful part of the Bible are simple to follow and cover an enormous range of human experience. One does not have to be a biblical scholar or a 'teacher' to explain the lessons of life that are contained there, and it does help, I have found, to use a simple, and easy-to-read version of the Bible.

In each of the first ten chapters of the Book of Proverbs, mention is made of the value of wise instruction from parents. Children are told to *'hear the instruction of their father, and forsake not the law of their mother'* (Proverbs 1:8). The word 'instruction' as it relates to the father, is straightforward in its meaning; that of simply teaching truths and principles. The word 'law' (torah) used for teaching from the mother however, is a little stronger, and implies lifestyle as well as verbal instruction. The hope that God had in Abraham, when He made him to be the father of His people, was based largely on the fact that Abraham would *'teach his children after him'* (Genesis 18:19).

In the first chapter of the Book of Proverbs, there is strong encouragement about the getting of this wisdom and instruction by children from parents.

> 2. *To know wisdom and instruction, to perceive the words of understanding,*
> 3. *To receive the instruction of wisdom, justice, judgment, and equity;*

4. *To give prudence to the simple, to the young man knowledge and discretion.*   Proverbs 1:2–4

Marriage

22. *Wives, submit to your own husbands, as to the Lord.*
23. *For the husband is head of the wife, as also Christ is head of the Church, and He is the Saviour of the body.*
Ephesians 5:22–23
(See also Colossians 3:18, and 1 Corinthians 11:3)

The above scriptures make it quite clear that the husband is to have *headship* in the home, under God. This headship is in no way to be a dominating one though, but must be exercised with the same sort of love that Christ has for His Church. If husbands truly loved their wives in this way, they would be easy to submit to, and marriage problems would almost totally disappear.

Role Responsibilities

Both the husband and the wife have different role functions to perform in a marriage. God has set things in order so that there is true partnership and cooperation in the marriage relationship, just as there is in the Godhead. The Bible says that the Father, the Word, and the Spirit *agree in one* (1 John 5:7–8).

This truth brings out the real reason for authority. *The real reason for authority in the earth, is for **agreement** to be found on earth, concerning God's will in Heaven.* A husband is not to be *the boss*. He is the one who must give account to God that agreement has been reached together between husband and wife, concerning the will of God for their life decisions. In every relationship structure that is to be blessed by God, someone is held to account *by* God, for the *corporate or joint* decisions regarding direction and purpose and methods etc. that are pleasing *to* God.

The husband's role in marriage is *headship*, and the wife's role is *helper* (Genesis 2:18). Each role in a structured relationship has responsibilities, and if each person applies themselves to accept and abide by those responsibilities, then the relationship will work! The trouble with human nature (that's all of us) is that we are more concerned with what the *other person* should be doing, regarding *their* role responsibilities, than what *we* should be doing, so that we do not attend to our own responsibilities. And so there are the predictable breakdowns in relationships that occur.

The role responsibilities of the husband involved in *headship* are: *To love, to provide*, and *to exercise authority*. The role responsibilities of the wife involved in *helping*, are: *To respond, to sustain*, and *to influence*. We will look at the role responsibilities of the husband first.

The Husband's Role – Headship

1. To Love

We have seen that a husband is to love his wife as Christ loved the Church, and gave Himself for it (Ephesians 5:25). This love is a sacrificial love, or *agape* love, which means denying oneself and putting the other person first. God commands men to love in this way, because they have to learn to choose to do it. God did not command wives to love in this way – He didn't have to – because women have a capacity to demonstrate this kind of love in a far greater way than men do.

2. To Provide

Part of the judgement upon man because of the fall of Adam, was '*in the sweat of his face to eat bread*' putting upon the man the responsibility for *hard work* to earn his keep, and to provide for his family. This was to adjust the flaw in man which came to the surface in the time of temptation in the garden, which was, *to ignore the responsibility he should have been taking to protect and cover his wife from the serpent*. Being made the provider was now God's way of making the proper adjustment. This does not have to remain as some *curse* however, as Jesus has become the curse for us, and employment and career is now a wonderful opportunity to walk in the blessings of the Father.

3. To Exercise Authority

This is perhaps one of the most difficult lessons for men to learn (none of them are easy!). Men seem to have to put a lot of hard work into learning their proper role responsibilities, whereas women appear to be far better equipped by God to respond to their God-given assignment. Perhaps this is precisely because of the very dim view that God took of man, when man neglected to take his responsibility in the garden of Eden, by not protecting his wife from the serpent. But taking true authority is not something which comes naturally and it is of great significance that Jesus discipled *men* and taught them the lessons of authority in the Kingdom of God. They made a number of mistakes in the learning process, and one notable one was when James and John, the sons of Zebedee (Matthew 20:20–24), began to argue about who was to be 'greatest' in the Kingdom, and who was going to sit at the right hand and at the left, of Jesus in His Kingdom.

This was the opportunity for Jesus to teach them the true nature of Kingdom authority. They thought that authority meant *position*, and Jesus taught them that it meant *service*. He told them that in the world, those who had authority exercised dominion over them, but in His Kingdom it would not be so, but rather *'let he who is greatest among you be your servant'*. Jesus demonstrated this kind of authority and became *'KING OF KINGS'*. This kind of 'serving authority' includes, *understanding teamwork, inspiring those around you, taking initiative, being decisive, and giving account.*

The Wife's Role – Helper

1. To Respond

Just as the husband is to love, so the wife is to respond. It is a commonly known and well observed fact that women respond to God easier than men do. They are usually the prayer warriors in the church, and are more sensitive to human need, and they show compassion for the feelings of others. One explanation for the difficulty that men have to responding to God, where women don't is that they are in some kind of 'male to male' competition with Him, whereas women have no such problem, and in fact are drawn to Him more naturally. This natural response is one of *trust* in God's character and strength, *and this is true submission*. Remember the story of Jack and Jill, back in chapter two? When Jack exercised the faith in God to *love* Jill, He demonstrated the strength and authority that made Jill feel secure and able to respond to him. A woman's response to her husband, in submission, is helped greatly by her first submitting and responding to God, and trusting Him to strengthen her husband.

2. To Sustain

Again, we see two parts working together to make up the whole. We just saw how loving and responding work together. Now we see how *providing* and *sustaining* work together. Proverbs chapter thirty-one gives an account of a woman whose value is 'far above rubies'. She is one who is very resourceful and is able to take what is provided and make it meet the needs of her household. There is also the role of 'emotionally sustaining' that a woman can exercise in a beautiful way. Witness the way the women sustained Jesus in his hour of suffering and sorrow. Where were the men at the foot of the cross? (Except for John, a very sensitive man.)

3. To Influence

A woman has the same influence in the Kingdom of God as a man, even though the functional role of *government* is different. This means that there is the same anointing, power, and gifting available through the Holy Spirit for the work of God to be done. This place of influence enjoys however, a place of protection and covering from man, in God's order, as it was meant to be in the beginning, in the garden of Eden. Therefore room must be given, and initiative must be taken, for the wisdom, discernment, and faith, and whatever else God provides, to work together as man and woman to do the will of God.

The Church

Here, as in all of God's other structured relationships, there is an order to be observed, so that the will of God can be done together in the community of saints, in agreement. Elders are told to shepherd the flock of God, over which He has given oversight (1 Peter 5:2). Special honour is to be given to elders who 'rule well' (1 Timothy 5:17), and other ministries, such as *apostles, prophets, evangelists, pastors, and teachers*, are placed by God, in the Church, *'for the equipping of the saints for the work of the ministry'*.

> 7. *Remember those who rule over you, who have spoken the word of God to you, whose faith follow, considering the outcome of their conduct.*
> 17. *Obey those who rule over you, and be submissive, for they watch out for your souls, as those who must give account. Let them do so with joy, and not with grief, for that would be unprofitable for you.*
>
> Hebrews 13:7, and 17

This place of authority in the Church is one of grave responsibility, and as seen in the scriptures above in the book of Hebrews, requires that these people *speak the word of God, have a faith that can be followed, have a conduct that must be considered, must watch for souls, and must give account.*

Employment

God worked. He was the most creative and productive worker of all time. Everything He created, He evaluated, and pronounced it 'good'. The first chapter of the Book of Genesis is the record of God's working week. It was a good week, and a lot of work was done by God in that week, however long the 'days' were. That was the week that was! In that week, God established the pattern for all work. Firstly, all work is a privilege, not a curse, because God worked and enjoyed it! And therefore all work should be enjoyable, creative, and productive, and all work should be *evaluated – To see if it is good.* That is why an authority structure exists in *the area of work and employment, to evaluate and make payment for the work done. The Word of God tells us what that authority structure is.*

3:22. Servants obey in all things your masters according to the flesh, not with eyeservice, as men-pleasers, but in sincerity of heart, fearing God.

23. And whatever you do, do it heartily, as to The Lord and not to men,

24. knowing that from the Lord you will receive the reward of the inheritance; for you serve the Lord Christ.

25. But he who does wrong will be repaid for the wrong which he has done, and there is no partiality.

4:1. Masters, give your servants what is just and fair, knowing that you also have a Master in heaven.

Colossians 3:22–4:1
(see also Ephesians 6:6–9. 1 Timothy 5:18)

So, as employees, and employers, we must be willing to work in agreement for what is good and productive. If this were done scripturally there would be no union strife, and nations, as well as individuals would prosper.

The State

1. Let every soul be subject to the governing authorities. For there is no authority except from God, and the authorities that exist are appointed by God.

2. Therefore whoever resists the authority resists the ordinance of God, and those who resist will bring judgement on themselves.

3. For rulers are not a terror to good works, but to evil. Do you want to be unafraid of the authority? Do what is good, and you will have praise from the same.

Romans 13:1–4

The conflict between Church and State has been an age-old one that has gone on for centuries, and many theories have been put forward for the correct distinction between State and Ecclesiastical authority. The problem is solved simply when it is realised that there does not have to be a conflict, as long as people know that Church and State can exist, side by side, as separate entities in themselves, both under the authority of God, because they both serve different purposes.

The Church exists as God's authority structure for the sanctification of society on earth. The State exists for the upholding of law and order – that is why they *'bear not the sword* (these days 'the gun'), *in vain'*, referring to the magistrates and police. The Church cannot put people into gaol, or execute them for wrong doing (though attempts have been made by the Church to 'police' God's people). But the State *is* God's instrument for the keeping of law and order, and for this reason we pay taxes. As the scripture says, 'Tribute to whom tribute is due'. God will *always* work through an authority structure, according to *the fifth commandment* – Honour your father and your mother', so as to check the unrestrained behaviour of human nature. Much unnecessary and harmful effort has been put in by the Church to run the State, and much unnecessary effort has been put in by the State, to run the Church, when *both* must be seen as being 'run by God' for His purposes.

Resistance to Authority

In the last chapter we saw that disobedience to the commandment of 'resting in the sabbath' resulted in frustration and anxiety in the life. This frustration and anxiety causes *resistance* to all forms of authority. This is because a self determined life wants to resist any form of outside influence or control. This self determined person sees authority as a threat, and the behaviour that follows may fall into one of the three following categories: *Escaping authority, destroying authority, and usurping authority (or taking-over authority)*.

1. Escaping Authority
Those who seek to escape authority fall into another two categories, *the rebel*, and *the drop-out*.

(a) The Rebel. The rebel despises authority and in his attempts to be seen to be free from authority, will usually try to find ways of making an open show of despising authority. He will do this often through provocative behaviour such as, *offensive language, unconventional dress and appearance, and the abusing of privilege.*

The rebel will often associate himself with causes that seem 'anti-authority'. The truth is that a true rebel will have no commitment to *any cause* because of the discipline and the coming under of authority that would be necessary. The true rebel sees causes as outlets for demonstrating his real resistance to authority. The tragedy is that he becomes a pawn in a chess game of power, used by the manipulators to whom the causes really matter. The scriptures call him 'the scorner'.

(See Proverbs 1:22; 3:34; 9:7, 8; 13:1; 14:6; 21:11; 21:24.)

(b) The Drop-out. The drop-out resents authority because of its challenge to his idleness. He wants to escape authority so that he can be left to his selfishness. The drop-out, like the rebel, will often *also* indulge in *offensive behaviour (if it gratifies his lusts), unconventional dress and appearance (out of laziness), and the abusing of privilege (out of inconsideration).* The drop-out, unlike the rebel, will never be seen aligning himself to causes, since all he wants is a totally self-determined and self-centred life free from all outside influence. In this he is like what the scriptures call 'the sluggard'.

(See Proverbs 6:6; 10:26; 13:4; 20:4; 26:16.)

2. Destroying Authority

Those who seek to destroy authority also fall into *two more categories*. These are, *the subversive*, and *the seditious*.

(a) The Subversive. This person tries to control things 'from behind'. He does not want to take over, or lead from in front, but instead wants to remove the obstacle of authority because it stops him from getting his own way. He always thinks he is right, and is mostly unaware or uncaring of the chaos that he causes, but is able to get other people 'on-side' with him. He does not respect authority, and so lacks integrity, showing the attributes of a 'fool' in the scriptures.

> *The way of a fool is right in his own eyes, but he who heeds counsel is wise.*   Proverbs 12:15

(b) The Seditious. This person seeks to destroy authority by using the weapons of criticism and divisiveness. The seditious thrives on the strategy of exposing the weaknesses of people in

authority. Ham, Noah's son was an example of this in the Book of Genesis when he exposed his father's nakedness, when Noah was drunken and naked in his tent.

> *And Ham the father of Canaan, saw the nakedness of his father and told his two brothers outside.*
>
> Genesis 9:22

Paul warned against the seditious person in the letter to the Romans.

> 17. *Now I urge you, brethren, note those who cause divisions and offences, contrary to the doctrine which you have learned, and avoid them.*
> 18. *For those who are such do not serve our Lord Jesus Christ, but their own belly, and by smooth words and flattering speech deceive the hearts of the simple.*
>
> Romans 16:17–18

3. Usurping Authority

Those who usurp or try to take-over authority, also fall into two categories, which are, *the tyrant*, and *the position seeker*.

(a) The Tyrant. The tyrant is a person who is *already in a position of authority*, but he abuses his place of authority, and so therefore is in rebellion to God's authority.

Our examples of this in scripture are *most* of the kings of Israel and Judah.

> 11. *And he said, 'This will be the behaviour of the king who will reign over you: He will take your sons and appoint them for his own chariots, to be his horsemen ...*
> 18. *'And you will cry out in that day because of your king whom you have chosen for yourselves, and the Lord will not hear you in that day.'*   1 Samuel 8:11, 18

(b) The Position Seeker. This person sees a place of security and self determination in getting for himself a place of authority. He is not interested in making decisions that will benefit other people, even though he will sometimes manipulate

people to agree with him concerning a 'worthy cause' and so justify his self exaltation. An example in scripture is Adonijah.

> *Now Adonijah, the son of Haggith, exalted himself, saying, 'I will be king', and he prepared for himself chariots and horsemen, and fifty men to run before him.*
>
> 1 Kings 1:5

God's Dealing on Rebellion

The judgement on all forms of rebellion is being inflicted with inferiority (Ham's descendants were made 'servants of servants'), or cast down from their place, if they have one. Examples of this are Lucifer (Isaiah 14:12–14), and Nebuchadnezzar (Daniel 4:30–33). Where redemption is possible (which counts Lucifer out), the dealing is meant to show a person the value of trusting another to influence their life.

Chapter 7

Live and Let Love

The Sixth Commandment

You shall not murder.   Exodus 20:13

We can see that this commandment speaks about more than just the act of taking of life in general, but is concerned with the heart attitude of malice, or the intention to let hatred or some other hurtful and evil passion harm another person. Jesus enlarged on this commandment in the sermon on the mount.

> 21. *'You have heard that it was said to those of old, "You shall not murder." And whoever murders will be in danger of the judgement.*
> 22. *'But I say to you that whoever is angry with his brother without a cause shall be in danger of the judgement. And whoever says to his brother "Raca!" shall be in danger of the council. But whoever says, "You fool!" shall be in danger of hell fire.*
> 23. *'Therefore if you bring your gift to the altar, and there remember that your brother has something against you,*
> 24. *'Leave your gift there before the altar, and go your way. First be reconciled to your brother, and then come and offer your gift.*   Matthew 5:21–24

Care for Life and Relationships

In the last commandment, concerning our relationship with authority, we saw that the problem in the people that God was dealing with, was the inability to trust another person to influence or direct their life. This was because of suspicion and self determination, so that they could have their own way. And now we see that the person who has a suspicion and mistrust of authority, will pass this suspicion and mistrust on to others, and, still determined to have their own way, will behave in a way that is destructive of all relationships.

In the above scripture, Jesus is interpreting the spirit of the sixth commandment, and takes its meaning beyond just the taking of life, and brings it into the area of *emotional control*, concerning our feelings towards other people. The two main thoughts which He mentions are *malice on the one hand*, and *reconciliation* on the other.

1. *Malice* is having a destructive heart of anger towards another person, which expresses itself in angry insults and threats. These insults and threats have the effect of 'killing' a relationship and causing a separation between friends or acquaintances (and very often, family). Usually the reason for this malice is that the angry person is being made angry because they are not getting their own way in a matter, because of what someone else is doing or saying to get in the way. A person can get angry with another also, because of how they are made to 'feel' by that other person. They may be made to feel guilty, or inadequate, or rejected (remember Jack and Jill again?), and so let out their negative and destructive feelings upon that other person, instead of being in control of their emotions. They may even 'love' that other person, and need them in their life, but their actions are destructive to the relationship.

2. The heart of a *reconciler* wants to see relationships built up and not destroyed. A reconciler is inclusive towards others, and devotes himself to *establishing, maintaining*, and *restoring* relationships.

(a) Establishing relationships. This is done by having an attitude of acceptance toward others. This is why it is important to accept ourselves as we are, so that we too, can accept others as *they* are. Many people make a big fuss about what the differences are between them, and base their acceptance of others on whether they hold the same point of view as themselves. We were accepted by God, in Christ, when we were in

opposition to God. The Word speaks to us about the ministry of reconciliation of Jesus towards us.

> *That is, that God was in Christ reconciling the world to Himself, not imputing their trespasses to them, and has committed to us the word of reconciliation.*
>
> 2 Corinthians 5:19

(b) *Maintaining Relationships*. Most relationships fail through either no communication, or bad communication. Some people can make friends easily, but then treat them casually or indifferently, by not maintaining proper communication. This allows misunderstandings and even suspicions to arise and weaken the relationship. The Word of God in Ephesians chapter four and verse twenty nine tells us to let *'no corrupt communication proceed out of your mouth, but what is good for necessary edification ...'*

(c) *Restoring Relationships*. We were brought back into relationship with God, through the forgiveness we received through the cross of Christ. This was the act of reconciliation that made us *one* with God. This is also the act of faith and love that we can exercise, as Christians, through the cross in *our* lives, in forgiving others their offences and so restoring relationships. We will deal with the nature of offences, and the management of them, later in this chapter.

Retaliation

Jesus' whole life was a testimony to the principle of non-retaliation. When He was 'reviled' (or insulted), He did not 'revile in return ...' (1 Peter 2:23). He spoke strongly against retaliation between God's children with one another, and with other people also, outside the family of God.

> 38. *'You have heard that it was said, "An eye for an eye, and a tooth for a tooth."*
> 39. *'But I tell you not to resist an evil person. But whoever slaps you on your right cheek, turn the other to him also.*
> 43. *'You have heard that it was said, "you shall love your neighbour and hate your enemy."*

44. *'But I say to you, "love your enemies, bless those who curse you, do good to those who hate you, and pray for those who spitefully use you and persecute you."'*

Matthew 5:38–39, 43–44

In telling us not to retaliate, and to love our enemies, Jesus is *not* saying that we must not protect ourselves or those under our protection from destruction. Even the laws of the land are against retaliation, but allow self defence. If I were to stop a thief or a murderer in the act of a crime, and cause him bodily harm in the act of my restraint against him, in saving my own or another's life or property, then I would be judged by man and by God, as acting in responsible self defence. This is not retaliation, or *'an eye for an eye'*. This is also not sinning against *'turning the other cheek'*.

It would be retaliation and sinning against turning the other cheek however, if I chased the man up the street and caused him bodily harm out of a motive of revenge and retaliation. We are not allowed to take the law into our own hands and *'punish the evil doer'*, as this is what the State is given authority by God to do (Romans 13:4).

When Jesus quoted the scripture from Leviticus chapter twenty-four and verse thirty, concerning *'an eye for an eye and a tooth for a tooth,'* He was also looking to make an adjustment to their corrupt interpretation of their own scriptures. That scripture was written *not to demand retaliation of an eye for an eye etc.* but to restrain them from exacting *more* than their fair share of justice, according to fairness and equity. For instance, instead of being repaid an ox for the accidental killing of their ox, they would demand a higher payment, and oppress one another, if they had the force or influence to do so. Instead, the scribes had made this precept a rule of retaliation.

The Death Penalty

The Word of God is clear that those who murder others, that is, cause death with malicious intent, are to be put to death by society.

'Whoever sheds man's blood, By man his blood shall be shed; for in the image of God He made man.

Genesis 9:6

This scripture states both the command or injunction that God gives to man regarding the punishment against the sanctity of life, and the *reason* for the punishment. *The reason is not retaliation.* The reason is that man is made in God's image, and therefore *life is sacred! Any exercise of a death penalty for a reason other than this is not scriptural.*

That is why today, there is such confusion regarding the death penalty. Today we see, on the one hand murderers getting away with murder, abortionists killing millions per year, and the elderly in danger of having their lives terminated because of non-productivity. On the other hand we see a blood lust for revenge on murder-rapists, and lynch mobs calling for the death penalty to be returned. If the death penalty were to be returned for the reasons most people want it to be, it would be almost as bad as the crimes it was supposed to judge.

The confusion about the sanctity of life today is a direct result of a misunderstanding of what 'sanctity' means. The meaning of the word comes from the idea of protecting what is *God's.* Man has changed it into the protecting of what is *his,* and what he has strong feelings about, if and when it suits him, and there are some more concerned with saving whales and trees these days for their own values, than for truly caring for God's creation. If we relate to God, we will relate to His creation.

The Handling of Offences

Jesus came down to earth to live as a human being, and He knew perfectly the human condition. He knew that people would become offended at one another and that fights and wars would start because of this. A person gets offended when they do not see the behaviour, or get the treatment that they were expecting from another. This is more than mere disappointment, and the fault can be with either party, or both. People became offended at Jesus, but it was not His fault. He just did not always do what people expected Him to do *for them.*

> *'Woe to the world because of offences! For offences must come, but woe to that man by whom the offence comes!'*
> Matthew 18:7

Lucifer was the first person to be offended, and he has been carrying the offence ever since! He wanted to be like God, and to take the glory and worship due to God alone. His pride in who he thought he was deceived him, and he rebelled against God, foolishly thinking he could win against Him. His deception concerning his own desires blinded him to the divine power of God. The same thing happens with man, and the first thing we do to God, or even to one another is become blinded to God's divine power, even as it works through the anointing in others.

In the book of Numbers in chapter twelve, Aaron and Miriam, the brother and sister of Moses, became offended at Moses for marrying an Ethiopian woman. In their offence, and their deception, they immediately began to compare themselves with Moses, despising the divine calling and appointment that God had put upon his life. Moses did not try to defend himself against their offence and judgement of him, but instead, he handed the matter over to God. This was true meekness, and God judged Aaron and Miriam severely.

John The Baptist became offended with Jesus at one time. The account of the incident is in Matthew 11:2–6.

> 2. *And when John had heard in prison about the works of Christ, he sent two of his disciples*
> 3. *and said to Him, 'Are You the Coming One, or do we look for another?'*
> 4. *Jesus answered and said to them, 'Go and tell John the things which you hear and see:*
> 5. *'The blind receive their sight and the lame walk; the lepers are cleansed and the deaf hear; the dead are raised up and the poor have the gospel preached to them.*
> 6. *And blessed is he **who is not offended because of Me.**'*
> Matthew 11:2–6

Note carefully that Jesus did **not** say, *'and I'm setting the prisoners free!'*

This is what John expected of Jesus. He was a prophet, and he knew what Jesus, the Messiah had been sent to do – he had read it in Isaiah, and Jesus had just quoted it – but Jesus had left out the part about the prisoners, and John was offended, *because John was in prison and he wanted to get out*. But this was not to be the will of the Lord. So Jesus told John's disciples to tell John not to be offended. And the point to note is, that John immediately despised the anointing of Jesus when he became offended, and asked if he should *'look for another.'* *Suspicion and mistrust come easily when we are offended.*

Defence Mechanisms

God has created within man a most wonderful built-in defence mechanism for survival against physical destruction. He has *not*, however, given to man a built-in defence mechanism to cope with emotional pressure, because He is our defence in that area. The built-in defence against physical destruction is, as I have said, wonderful in its complexity and efficiency. The body is able to produce antibodies against infection, and to reject foreign matter from within its own cell structure. Even in times of imminent danger, the body will release chemicals and hormones to get the blood pumping harder to the heart and muscle system, in order to be ready to take flight, and react effectively to danger.

But this has no parallel in the emotions. God has not equipped us with any 'hormones' or 'antibodies' against rejection, or disapproval, or criticism, or any other hurtful thing that we might suffer at the hands of another person. God has given Himself to us, to trust, and to defend us in the final outcome, as he did for Moses, and for His Son, Jesus. Even though He suffered death on the cross, He received the eternal and final payment of justice in His resurrection, and glory.

He said this first to Abraham, and then to David, and He says it to us.

> … *Do not be afraid Abraham, I am your shield, and your exceeding great reward.* Genesis 15:1

> *But The Lord has been my defence, and My God the rock of my refuge.*   Psalm 94:22

Nevertheless, we begin to fashion our own defence mechanisms against the pressures of life. Some of these defences are minor ones and fairly harmless ones, more in the line of 'stress relieving' activities, such as biting fingernails, or chewing gum, or other habits. But there is a line that must be drawn when these defence mechanisms become harmful and do damage to ourselves, not only physically, but also emotionally, as they can bring on guilt, and shame, and cause great damage to relationships. If these are not checked, we start to 'fall apart' as a person, and 'disintegrate', losing our integrity. A classic case is a dependence on alcohol or drugs, to take away the pressures of life.

Relational Defences

The most subtle and dangerous of our defence mechanisms are those behavioural ones that we use as weapons or as shields against other people. We will deal with the three major areas next. These are: *Withdrawal, resistance*, and *aggression*.

(a) Withdrawal. This person gets their defence mechanism from the snail, or the turtle, and whether they do so consciously or not, they have developed the habit of withdrawing into their shell, whenever they are threatened by circumstances that *require a change of will*. This eventually destroys relationships, and makes them even *more* vulnerable to feeling threatened by the circumstances of life, because they make it extremely difficult for their former friends to approach them.

These people are often sulky, sullen, and incommunicative, and are able to justify their behaviour to themselves by claiming that they are 'misunderstood.'

(b) Resistance. These people are not so much like the snail or the turtle, but are more like the 'hedgehog', or 'porcupine', which has spikes coming out from it to protect it from anyone coming near it. They can also be likened to a kicking mule who thinks that you are going to make it do something it does not want to do. These people are often stubborn and obstinate, and

are *determined* not to change for anybody. Even close friends, whom they love, often cannot approach them.

> *Do not be like the horse or like the mule, Which have no understanding, Which must be harnessed with bit and bridle, Else they will not come near you.*   Psalm 32:9

(c) Aggression. The aggressive person defends themselves by being 'hot headed' and quick tempered. They see any challenge in a relationship as a personal threat and have to retaliate. They are often very sorry later – when it is too late and the damage has been done, but they feel a strong sense of self righteousness at the time of their aggression which blinds them to the feelings of others, or the true justice of the situation.

These people can become dogmatic, self opinionated, and quick to judge, and are what the Bible often refers to as 'a striker'. These people are therefore disqualified from holding office in the Church.

> *For a bishop must be blameless, as a steward of God, not self-willed, not quick tempered ...*   Titus 1:7

In the second Book of Samuel, in chapter sixteen, and verses five to thirteen, David is accosted by an aggressive person called Shimei. This man cursed David as he rode along, and threw stones at him, from a hillside opposite him, accusing him of being a man of blood. David's companions, who were riding on his right and on his left hand side, wanted to take off Shimei's head, saying – *'why should this dead dog curse the king?'*. But David showed a Godly restraint and meekness, and replied to his men along the lines of: 'If God has sent this man to tell me what I'm really like, then I cannot destroy him for that, and on the other hand, if God has not sent him, then God will deal with the matter and even repay me good for this cursing of me today.'

Defences and Depression

When our defence mechanisms are over-used, we become emotionally fatigued, because we have not been trusting God as our defence, and so have used up our own reserves, to no real effect. Anything that is overused becomes fatigued, even metal. But the effect of emotional fatigue in human beings, be they Christians or not, is depression. In fact that is the *basic cause of depression in people today*. The first sign of this depression coming in is a moodiness which cannot be explained, and which seems to happen for no reason. Then come the depression, and the colour goes out of life.

Then comes more distressing signs, such as fears that seem to come from nowhere, of being alone, or in closed spaces, or open spaces, or of other strange things. *The answer for any kind of fatigue is rest*. This is where God wants His child to rest in Him and trust Him for their defence and begin to believe that He has our safety and eternal security in His heart. As we re-establish our proper faith relationship with Him, we can begin to rest in Him and to love others instead of defending ourselves against them, and we begin to get healed from the fatigue and depression.

The judgement of God upon people who refuse to come to Him at these times, but rather use their defences to destroy relationships, is the same as the judgement God gave to Cain, when he murdered his brother. God isolated Cain from Himself and from others. This judgement was more than Cain could bear. This judgement serves to heighten, to an intolerable level, the experience of loneliness and alienation that people go through because they sin against love and trust. By sinning against love, they are cut off from love.

Release from Defensiveness

To be released from a life of defensiveness we must first return to trusting the love of God for us. As we believe in this love, we can unite our hearts to His in His care for others. Because these commandments are linked up to one another in a sequence, then it follows that there would be a failure somewhere in a person being able to properly relate to authority, as we have already seen. In the area of retaliation and defences, it also follows that a person would need to adjust their attitude of defensiveness towards authority, perhaps to God, or to parents, or to others in authority that have affected their lives in any way. In this way there can be *forgiveness* and where possible, reconciliation.

Chapter 8

Till Death (or whatever) do us Part

The Seventh Commandment

You shall not commit adultery Exodus 20:14

Adultery can be strictly defined as 'unlawful sexual intercourse with married people'. The commandment itself, and the 'spirit' of adultery takes a lot more into account however, and deals with the whole sphere of unfaithfulness, lust, and betrayal in relationships. As in the last commandment, Jesus once again expanded on this commandment in the sermon on the mount.

> 27. '*You have heard that it was said to those of old, "You shall not commit adultery."*
> 28. '*But I say to you that whoever looks at a woman to lust for her has already committed adultery with her in his heart.*' Matthew 5:27–28

The Turning Point

The seventh commandment can be called a turning point, because it is at this point of failure in relationships, that a person begins to treat other people as objects for self gratification (or obstacles *to* self gratification), rather than as people of great worth and value, and with feelings. The last commandment dealt with the value and the sanctity of life and relationships, and the breakthrough for a person failing in that commandment came through wholeheartedly embracing the love of God, through Jesus Christ, and therefore putting aside mistrust and suspicion, first of all to God, then to other people.

This meant accepting God's values for forgiveness, and acceptance (which is more than just mere tolerance). By doing this we were able to have the capacity formed in us, through God's grace, of exercising *emotional control* in our relationships, and refraining from anger and sullenness and other forms of destructive behaviour. This capacity to care overcomes the impulse to destroy, and releases a desire to build and preserve our relationships.

If however, this capacity is not developed in us, we become self centred. This shallowness in the life eventually leads to unfaithfulness. Materialism has replaced altruism.

The Options

The defensive attitudes mentioned in the last chapter end up cutting people off from one another, and this inner loneliness leaves a vacuum which has to be filled by something. It is at this point that a person has to make some choices. There are two major options from which to choose.

The option God wants a person to take is for them to cease from defensive behaviour, by letting the love of God flow through them to others. Then we can restore any broken relationships, and to begin to find the fulfilment and purpose that comes through living this way, in partnership with Jesus, and those He has placed with us.

The other option is to try and fill this vacuum by seeking self gratification. Only love can truly satisfy – and if a person cannot be *satisfied*, he will opt for being *gratified*. This second option is called *selfish desire, or lust*, and of course, leads to sin.

> 14. *But each one is tempted when he is drawn away by his own desires and enticed.*
> 15. *Then, when desire has conceived, it gives birth to sin; and sin, when it is full-grown, brings forth death.*
>
> James 1:14–15

The root of this sin is the need produced by the absence of

love. This can be seen operating even in early childhood, if the love and affection so needed in a child's life is badly neglected, and the child begins even then to seek out ways to gratify this need by looking for different ways to get comfort, emotionally and physically. Being emotionally deprived is usually compensated for by some kind of sensual, or physical gratification, and it is at this point that the life can become *predisposed*, though not yet occupied with, such things as over-eating, masturbation, and other comfort substitutes, which are often compulsive.

The drive to gratify and comfort oneself by way of compensation can usually be found in one of the following three categories: *sensual gratification, non-sensual gratification*, and *promiscuous relationships*.

1. Sensual Gratification
Sensual gratification is that kind of comfort that is used as a substitute for a loving relationship, whereby a person indulges themselves in some kind of physical pleasure which may be either *sexual* or *non-sexual*.

(a) Sexual
In this area are found such activities as masturbation, fornication, homosexuality, pornography, and there are probably a number of other perversions that do not need to be listed. But in counselling people that have been in bondage to such activities, it has been a consistent factor that the person has been through some kind of 'wilderness' in their experiences of deep and warm family or personal relationships. They have also often found a barrenness in normal friendships, where they can pour their heart out and let someone whom they trust, share their feelings with them.

And this may not have always been the case through all their lives. There may have been times when there were those strong family ties and bonds, and friendships, but through misfortune and other circumstances, there occurred separation, and the vacuum appeared, that only real relationships can fill. It has been at these moments, when a person is seeking a true remedy for this sickness of the soul, that the warmth and love of a true friend and Saviour, Jesus, can flood into the life. Walking with Him, a renewed individual can begin to weave together the threads of love and care in the wholesome regard and response to the people around him, and the fabric of his life becomes strong in grace and goodness. This person can put behind him forever the guilt and shame associated with the activities of the past.

(b) Non-Sexual

In this area are found such activities as over-eating, thrill-seeking, and drug abuse (which includes alcoholism, and the abuse of prescription drugs, such as tranquillisers, as well as the abuse of narcotics, and mind-expanding hallucinogenics).

At first glance, these pursuits and activities might seem to be rather 'private' habits, which do not involve causing harm to other people, only one's own self. But on reflection however, it is easy to see that not only does one destroy oneself in these activities but entire families, and communities, and societies are being destroyed because of the way relationships are destroyed in the process. The strange contradiction in people caught in these prisons of self destruction, is that while they seem to be morbidly interested in themselves, and no-one else, they cannot actually relate to themselves at all, and do not see themselves as they really are.

Within this very contradiction lies the answer to their problem. It is when a person is given a revelation of who they really are, especially in relationship to God through Jesus, as the object of His deep love and care, that they are motivated to be the person that they were created to be. The guilt associated with these self indulgences sets up a vicious cycle. First, there is the guilt experienced because of the lack of self control, and this brings on depression and remorse, and often self pity. Unfortunately people find comfort within this cycle, by going back to the means of self indulgence again, and so it goes on. To love and be loved for who they really are, and could be, is the real need in the life, but of course, this needs commitment to a relationship, and the commitment is just not there.

The road back seems too long, and all up hill, but in fact *all that is required is one decision*. That decision is one to *commit oneself to a relationship*, because, somewhere, at some time, that is what went missing or was never allowed to be formed.

User Pays
At this point it is worth mentioning the enormous cost to human life and resources that these last two areas of sensual gratification demand, both the sexual and the non-sexual expressions. If the devil wanted to shipwreck the human race, he could not have picked a better strategy to exhaust it of its lifeblood than through the seventh commandment, and especially through the tactic of sensual gratification as a substitute for loving, committed relationships.

The ravages of the disease of AIDS is of plague proportions that compares to anything that history has ever seen, and is getting worse by the day (without a cure!). Then there is the gigantic problem facing society today because of broken marriages, and homeless and neglected children. We haven't mentioned the financial cost of all of this yet either! But add to this the massive trade in pornography in books, magazines, films and videos, and we see that Satan has found the weak spot in human nature – *commitment to relationships*.

We have not mentioned yet either, the inflated dollar that inflates the belly with junk food, and then offers an inflated discount price on a weight loss program!

Let us now add a few billion dollars for alcohol abuse, not to mention the 'astro-dollar' that the drug and narcotic trade reaps – that one is just too big, even for people who exaggerate with statistics. All this, because of lack of commitment, should make any committed Christian committed to getting people committed, with a renewed sense of commitment!

2. Non-sensual Gratification
In this category there are the people who are not given to indulging themselves sensually, primarily for the kind of comfort that they can get to make up for a lack, or deprival, of love. These ones look rather to an exalted sense of achievement or even of self righteousness to gratify their lack of satisfaction in relationships, and to fill the vacuum that is left because of that lack.

This can be a very deceiving form of self gratification because it seems to occupy itself with things that can gain approval from most people, because of the emphasis that most people put on the outward appearance of things these days, and the performances that get approval from people generally.

In fact these following examples of self indulgence, *at the sake of a committed relationship*, are extremely *anti-social* in their outcome, and include such labels as: the workaholic, the compulsive hobbyist, the sporting fanatic, the insensitive 'do-gooder', and the religious obsessive.

These people may not seem to be 'committing adultery', but they are in fact *betraying a relationship* by putting their own obsession or fixation in front of those who want to be near and dear to them. Sometimes those 'near and dear' decide to give up, because the competition is too strong from the fixation that has swallowed up the life of that husband, or father, or wife, or mother. They have found another 'mate'.

We may tend to denounce the workaholic husband here as the number one suspect to be blamed, and indeed there are a lot of them. But we must not forget how subtle can be the alienation that a man feels because of a 'religious' wife. Marriage is special and sacred to God, and encouragement is given in the scriptures, in I Peter chapter three and in I Corinthians chapter seven, and in other places, for spiritual women to love and endear their husbands by their gracious femininity and loyalty.

The other areas speak for themselves, along the same lines, whether they be on sports-fields or in committee meetings of the Lion's Club. The characteristic feature of them all is a world that is created to fulfil the life of *one person*, even though other people may be involved to allow these activities to function.

3. Promiscuous Relationships

This would seem to be the most contradictory of all sins against involvement with relationships, because this deals with the person who is ever seeking to be involved at an emotional level with other people. The problem is that the promiscuous person uses the *experience* of the relationship (not valuing the other person for themselves), as an object of their self gratification.

They 'fall in love with love'. In other words, they confuse romance with relationship.

Because of this the promiscuous person is unable to maintain any lasting relationships, and is therefore seen as a butterfly flitting from one relationship to another.

Their obsession with 'deep and meaningful' relationships often compels them to excessively expose their inner thoughts to other new acquaintances that they might happen to be attracted to. This often invites a flush of instant attention, and is a stimulant for the promiscuous person, filling the vacuum temporarily, until at a later stage in that relationship – a *commitment* is called for –

> 'No more please! I wasn't in this for a commitment, just some relief from dissatisfaction.'

There is indeed a real place for sharing our hearts to one another, and even confessing our faults to one another. But this must be done with integrity, and not for attention seeking. The scriptural reason for this confessing of self to another is that '*you may be healed*' (James 5:16), and that healing is done within the sanctity of a caring and trusting relationship, and with faith. Of course there are other reasons for other kinds of intimate conversations to take place between close friends, and marriage partners, which are simply for the deepening of the relationship, and have nothing to do with faults or with healing, but the promiscuous does have this tendency to 'bare his soul' for the wrong reasons. Such people, by 'coming on strong' in the early stages of a relationship, produce in the other person a pressure of obligation to respond, which often weighs heavily upon them.

People with promiscuous hearts are the cause of much tension and confusion in marriages, where one, or both, partners have this problem. Even if a sexual offence never occurs to shake the marriage, the spirit of disloyalty and lack of true commitment is always there, weakening the effectiveness that an otherwise good marriage could have. This is because the commitment to marriage involves the *total life*, not merely a grudging abstinence from illicit sex.

Taking Advantage

I mentioned earlier the 'turning point' where materialism sets in and an 'adulterous' person sees other people as objects of, or obstacles to, their self gratification. There develops a growing sense of personal indifference in the personality of this type of person towards others. In counselling people caught in this web and whose marriages have broken down because of their infidelity, I have perceived in them a naive sense of right and wrong, like a distorted morality. I have even known them to pray that God would intervene and make a way for them to have what, or who, they desire. When confronted with the fact that sin is involved, their response is 'But God is forgiving isn't He?' What is happening is that immorality is becoming amorality.

I am pleased to say that I have seen a number of broken marriages restored (but still not enough), and in those that have been through the wounding and confusion of adultery to find repentance and restoration, there is the acknowledgment that they were 'blinded' to the reality of things. Before the repentance is received there is a deception and duplicity at work in their hearts, and it is at first not a deliberate one. They are genuinely convinced that life is meant to gratify them. There has been a shift in their value system, that makes them pursue their need for gratification with a cunning and fervour that nothing else in life can warrant.

Those who oppose them at this point and try to talk 'sense' to them are regarded as interfering and just not able to understand. It is then that the deliberate lying starts, and is excused, because people just 'don't understand.'

Taking advantage can take many other forms also, depending on the way people fail in this commandment. For instance Judas betrayed Jesus by trading Him for thirty pieces of silver, and that was a deception of a value system if ever there was one! Even Pontius Pilate betrayed Jesus by trading his office of trust as a magistrate for gaining favour with the Jews and Romans.

Open Shame

The judgement of God upon all forms of adultery or betrayal is open shame and disgrace. We see this in His dealings with His own people because of going after other gods, and betraying Him.

> 26. *Therefore I will uncover your skirts over your face, That your shame may appear.*
> 27. *I have seen your adulteries and your lustful neighings, the lewdness of your harlotry, Your abomination on the hills in the fields. Woe to you O Jerusalem! Will you still not be made clean?*   Jeremiah 13:26–27

The open shame can be seen to operate on the lives of those who have a lifestyle of adultery, when you observe how the media and the 'gossip columns' report on the most private details of their shame-filled lives. This is also the case of the military traitor who is put to open shame, not so much by the media, but on the parade ground and in front of his peers. This shame was meted out to the collaborators during wartime by the shaving of the head for open display in the community.

This experience of shame can cause people to see the real value of human dignity, and therefore respect it in the way that they should have. Peter the apostle was greatly shamed when he denied Jesus, but we see the faithfulness and loyalty of Jesus in restoring the repentant Peter.

> 15. *So when they had eaten breakfast, Jesus said to Simon Peter, 'Simon, son of Jonah, do you love Me more than these?' He said to Him 'Yes Lord, You know that I love You.' He said to him, 'Feed My lambs.'*
> 16. *He said again to him a second time, 'Simon, son of Jonah, do You love Me?' He said to Him, 'Yes Lord, You know that I love You.' He said to him, 'Tend My sheep.'*
> 17. *He said to him the third time, 'Simon, son of Jonah, do you love Me?' Peter was grieved because He said to him the third time, 'Do you love Me?' And he said to Him. 'Lord, You know all things. You know that I love you.' Jesus said to him, 'Feed my sheep.'*   John 21:15–17

It is a life changing revelation to know that Jesus is totally committed to, and believes in us, that the purpose for our lives can be fulfilled. Great is His faithfulness.

Chapter 9

Your Money or Your Life

The Eighth Commandment

You shall not steal.   Exodus 20:15

What are you Worth?

In the last commandment, which dealt with faithfulness and loyalty in relationships, we saw that materialism began to establish itself in the heart, so that things became more important than people. This shift of values makes itself evident in the behaviour of the person who is failing at a heart level in this way, in their relationships, because they start to devalue, not only relationships, but the actual *worth of people* generally.

The reason that this comes about is because the person who is failing in this way does not know how to *receive* from a true and faithful relationship – they have become independent of them for life fulfilment – and so if they are receiving nothing from them, then they are *worth* nothing to them. But in being unable to *receive*, this person has also developed a life pattern of having to *take*. To take from someone is totally different to receiving from someone. We can take something without having to bother about a relationship, or peoples' feelings, because we have become a *law unto ourselves*. But if we receive, we must have some kind of 'encounter' with the giver, so that we express gratitude and appreciation, not only for what has been given, but for who that person is. *That is what gives a person worth* in our eyes.

In receiving from another person properly, whether they are

giving us of their time, or service, or sympathy, or material goods, we are appreciating something else as well, at another level of respect for them, and that is the value of the effort and care that has gone into their giving. All of this goes into our valuation of a person, and their worth. The thief has lost this sense of value for people, in others, and in himself.

When is a Thief *Not a Thief?*

I once asked this question to a class of primary school students, and their answers were very entertaining, and some of them came close to answering correctly, but none of them could give the correct answer. Some of their answers included statements such as: 'When he goes to gaol,' or 'when he has got enough money.' A lot of them thought that the answer was 'when he stops stealing.' And this does seem like the obvious answer, but the scriptures tell us that a greater transformation is needed to change a thief from being a thief. Just as Jesus expanded on some of the commandments in the sermon on the mount, so the New Testament expands on the principles of certain commandments through the inspired writings of the apostles. Paul wrote concerning the transformation of a thief in Ephesians.

> *Let him who stole steal no longer, but rather let him labour, working with his hands what is good, that he may have something to give him who has need.*
>
> Ephesians 4:28

In expanding this scripture, and getting to the heart of the person who needs to be transformed by the truth of God's word, we can see that the total transformation is that *a taker becomes a giver*. And on the way to becoming a giver the thief also becomes *an honest worker*. The scope of this commandment then, is more than just a prohibition of stealing, but a change of heart that brings a person into the full understanding of their own, and other people's worth. The significant thing to see here, and which we will look at more closely later is that *a person's worth is linked to their giving*.

The scripture from Ephesians that has been quoted above actually covers three areas in our lives, which are: *Material honesty, productivity, and giving.*

1. Material Honesty

This issue deals with more than just the unlawful taking away of someone else's goods. It also refers to the whole sphere of respect and responsibility for that which belongs to others, including restitution for damage done accidentally, or through negligence. There are many ordinances found in The Old Testament which relate to the care of other people's property, and the restitution for damages done because of negligence. These ordinances are found in Exodus in chapters twenty-one and twenty-two, where it gives direction as to what to do if a man leaves a pit uncovered and a neighbour's ox or donkey falls into it, and dies. The man who dug the pit was obliged to pay the full market price for the dead animal and the dead animal became his own. If one man's ox harmed another man's ox so that it dies, then the owner of the live ox has to sell the live ox, and share the price of it with the owner of the dead ox, and they share the dead ox between them. But if however, it was common knowledge that the offending ox had been in the habit of goring before, and the owner had not kept it under control, then he had to pay ox for ox, and the dead animal became his own (Exodus 21:33–36).

These may appear to be boring trifles which do not deserve to be included in Holy Writ, but it demonstrates how much God values material honesty. In fact *volumes* of God's Word deal with such things as ownership, and stewardship, and borrowing and lending, the use and abuse of our talents, and giving and receiving. God does not do this just to give us handy hints on marketing, but He is relating our management of material things with our management of spiritual things.

> *'Therefore if you have not been faithful in the unrighteous mammon, who will commit to your trust the true riches?'*
> Luke 16:11

In the days of The Book of Exodus, when people had to

make restitution for injured cattle and other property (even human life in some instances), they had no 'general insurance scheme' to cover themselves, and because of the simplicity of the agricultural society in which they lived, there were sensible and realistic guidelines to follow. In the days in which we live, things are more complex. We do have insurance schemes, and a Christian should take a responsible attitude towards them, so that he is covered, not only for the stewardship of his own goods, but in the area of material honesty, for the respect of the property of other people as well.

2. Productivity

10. *For even when we were with you, we commanded you this: If anyone will not work, neither shall he eat.*

11. *For we hear that there are some who walk among you in a disorderly manner, not working at all, but are busybodies.*

12. *Now those who are such we command and exhort through our Lord Jesus Christ that they work in quietness and eat their own bread.*   2 Thessalonians 3:10–12

The Word of God here reveals that God requires us to be productive. We are told that we have to refrain from idleness and laziness. We are also not to presume upon others for our welfare, because we should recognise and appreciate the *worth* of another person's productivity. This principle applies to both those who employ other people to work for them, and also those who are under employment.

14. *You shall not oppress a hired servant who is poor and needy, whether one of your brethren or one of the aliens who is in your land within your gates.*

15. *Each day you shall give him his wages, and not let the sun go down on it, for he is poor and has set his heart on it; lest he cry out against you to the Lord, and it be sin to you.*
        Deuteronomy 24:14–15

17. *Let the elders who rule well be counted worthy of double honour, especially those who labour in the word and doctrine.*

18. *For the Scripture says, 'You shall not muzzle an ox while it treads out the grain,' and, 'The labourer is worthy of his wages.'*   1 Timothy 5:17–18

The Word of God is very strong concerning justice in the respect of the worth of a person's labour. The New Testament picks up the same theme in Ephesians chapter six, when it says employers have to treat their employees well, without threats, *'remembering that they and you have the same Master in Heaven, and there is no partiality with Him.'*

God is a worker and loves to work! He enjoyed creating us. When God created the world, He paused after each act of creation and evaluated what He had done, and saw that it was 'good.' That is why work is not a curse, but a blessing and a privilege, and God wants us to develop the correct attitude to it. This is why squandering and gambling is against God's work ethic. A gambler is willing to waste what has been earned by hard work, for the chance of getting more without working. The lesson of life shows us that gamblers do not win. The haunted look of the losing gambler is a picture of desperation, reflecting the sense of inner worthlessness that is being felt in the heart.

Similarly the squanderer has no regard for the worth of his own labours, or the labours of others. He sees productivity in terms of the 'benefit' it gives to him in being able to gratify himself with no regard for tomorrow, or for the needs of others. The scriptures link the squanderer (the waster or the 'destroyer') with the slothful. We see this in Proverbs 18:9.

He who is slothful in his work is a brother to him who is a great destroyer (waster).   Proverbs 18:9

The slothful or lazy person, sometimes called a 'sluggard' in the scriptures is always finding excuses (some of them quite outrageous, as you will see below) for not working, or for putting it off, till some other day – that never comes. The Book of Proverbs describes these people well.

The sluggard will not plow because of winter, therefore he will beg during the harvest and have nothing.

Proverbs 20:4

The slothful says, 'there is a lion in the road! A fierce lion is in the streets!'　　　　Proverbs 26:13

Outrageous!

As a door turns on its hinges, so does the slothful turn on his bed.　　　　Proverbs 26:14

The slothful man buries his hand in the bowl; It wearies him to bring it back to his mouth.　　　　Proverbs 26:15

3. Giving

God is a giver. He lives to give. He gave us life. The reason that life and death are two opposites is that one gives and the other takes away. In Jesus Christ, life overcame death at Calvary, and the power of the resurrection is to be seen in the lives of God's people. It can be witnessed in the way that they give of themselves, first to God and then to other people. I am not just talking about finances here, but of *ourselves*. The reason that God uses finances as an illustration so much in His Word, is that people place so much significant value and worth on what they possess. The truth is that we possess *nothing* – *everything belongs to God.*

The earth is the Lord's and all its fullness, the world and those who dwell therein.　　　　Psalm 24:1

It is because we acknowledge God's ownership of everything that we tithe to Him. Some people say that tithing belongs under the law of Moses, and therefore has been done away with in the New Testament. That is not true. Tithing began before Moses was born, and was first performed by Abraham, when he called God *'The possessor of Heaven and earth'* (Genesis 14:22). Tithing is an eternal principle that when exercised with faith, helps to change a 'taker' into a 'giver,' and releases faith for the provision of God in our lives.

*'Will a man rob God? Yet you have robbed Me! But you
say, "In what way have we robbed You?" In tithes and
offerings.'*   Malachi 3:8

Earlier on in this chapter, under the heading 'when is a thief
not a thief' I made a statement that said 'a person's worth is
linked to their giving.' I would like to expand on that statement
now.

In the above scripture from the Book of Malachi, we saw that
God expected His people to appreciate His worth, by paying
tithes. This was not because God needed the money! He owns
everything, as we saw in Psalm 24, that *'the earth is the Lord's,
and all its fullness.'* This can begin to give us an understanding
of what 'worth' relates to.

God is 'worth' everything. This is only *partly* because He
owns everything. The other factor is that God *gives* everything.
All that we have is from God, because He gave it to us. We
cannot *take* anything from God, it must be given. If someone
other than God owned *everything*, where would we stand in
regard to what we would have? (An impossible situation, but
let us just explore this thought for a moment.) It would all
depend upon what that 'owner' wanted to give to us. Perhaps if
we worked hard, he might pay us a set wage, perhaps a certain
amount of the air to breathe that he 'owned,' but certainly no
favours, like the fruit of the trees, or the minerals in the earth.
We would soon come to think of this new 'owner of the
universe' that he was not 'worth' much at all, because he could
give nothing. And that is why *God alone is worthy.*

Worship

The word 'worship' comes from an old English word called
'worthship', which said fairly clearly what it meant. It showed
that we have an attitude of worship to one who is 'worthy' in a
special sense. The principle here is that people have always
worshipped what they most value and think is most worthwhile to them. The subtle thing is that when a person worships
any other person than God, he gives ownership of himself to
that other person, and looks to them to receive what he needs
for his life.

111

That is why tithing is an act of worship, because by making that act of faith we are telling God that He is worth everything to us, and not just our job, or our bank account. All these are merely channels that God uses to release His provision. This is also why He wants us to be good stewards of what we have, because it measures how we look after His things.

When we acknowledge that God owns what we have, we can safely commit those things back to Him, knowing that if we have done our best to care for them, then He will do the rest of the caring and protecting of what He has given us. It is like putting what we 'own' on God's altar and consecrating it to Him. In the Second Book of Chronicles in chapter thirty-six, there is an account of how the precious treasures of the house of the Lord were taken by the Chaldeans and carried to Babylon. But those things had touched God's altar! Later on, when the captivity was finished, God sent for these precious things to be brought back to the House of The Lord, because, He said, *'they are holy unto Me.'*

I see the same thing happening to God's people today, especially with their children. When parents dedicate their children to the Lord in faith, acknowledging God's ownership of them, they become sanctified to Him (1 Corinthians 7:14). They have touched the altar. They may go through difficult times in their later years, but if they have been brought up in the way that they should go, there comes a time when God sends for them to return to Him. He wants them back in The House of The Lord.

Giving is Worthwhile

There is one who scatters, yet increases more; and there is one who withholds more than is right, but it leads to poverty. Proverbs 11:24

The first part of this scripture describes a faith principle that releases a miraculous increase of what is given out of a right heart. This *'one who scatters'* is a person who is bountiful in his giving. His experience can be likened to the account of the miraculous increase of the jar of oil and the measure of flour that the widow of Zarephath experienced when she gave of her last to the prophet Elijah. It can also be likened to the feeding of the multitude with the loaves and fishes by Jesus, when the little boy gave all that he had to eat for himself.

On the other hand the *'one who withholds'* can be likened to the hoarder who stops the flow of giving and receiving by withholding more than he should. Once people begin to withhold and hoard, then there is less left to go around for everybody. It can be likened to a fuel strike, when people rush to hoard fuel for themselves. There is suddenly a greater crisis than there was in the first place, because once the panic starts, most of the petrol gets hoarded in people's garages, rather than being used for the necessary purposes for which it was meant.

A thief was seen to be worthless in Israel, as seen in the consequences for the person who happened to kill him in the act of breaking and entering.

> *'If the thief is found breaking in, and he is struck so that he dies, there shall be no guilt for his bloodshed.'*
>
> Exodus 22:2

Jesus praised the sacrificial giving in the temple of the 'widow's mite.' He saw the higher value of her giving, over against the 'easy' giving of the rich, as a demonstration of her faith and trust in God's provision, and also of her true attitude of 'worship.'

God has given to each of us those things that we can give to others, and He is not measuring quantity but quality of giving. Some may not feel that they have much to give, and so they withhold, thinking that what they have is not 'worth' anything. These people have things around the wrong way. We are worth 'everything' to God, and He highly values that which we give to Him in our love and obedience to Him, and He is pleased when we share with others. It is worthwhile.

Chapter 10
Tell It Like It Is

The Ninth Commandment

You shall not bear false witness against your neighbour.

Exodus 20:16

The Big Lie

The first contact that man had with evil in the garden of Eden, was with the serpent, who told Eve a lie. It was not only 'a' lie it was 'the' lie. The lie was that if man disobeyed God he *'would not surely die'* (Genesis 3:4). This appealed to man's sense of independence, and led to the first act of independence, which is another word for pride, and caused man to rebel against God and become deceived by sin for the first time.

The first lie that was ever told on earth led to death, which demonstrates the *power* of what is called false witness. We will see in this chapter how the abuse of this *power* follows on logically from the problem that is dealt with in the last chapter, concerning stealing. Satan is called *'a liar and the father of it'* by Jesus (John 8:44) and the power he wields is based on his own self-deception and his deceiving of others.

In the last chapter we saw that stealing reflected the lack of worth that a thief felt for himself and other people. Therefore there was no regard for the value of a relationship with another person. The thief had become a taker and could not give, and if they did appear to be giving, it was always some kind of a trade for their own advantage. This attitude leads to a self determination that is altogether *lawless*. It is lawless because there is no regard for the regulations and sanctions regarding relationships, whereby we protect and care for one another. God regulates relationships. In fact that is about *all* He regulates, and the ten commandments are God's prescription for the regulation of relationships. Paul says that to love one another is the fulfilling of the whole law (Romans 13:8–10), and to completely disregard God's guidelines and regulations for what He sees as most valuable in life (our obedience to Him is based on relationship) is an act of wilful *lawlessness*.

The Power Game

Death and life are in the power of the tongue, and those who love it will eat its fruit. Proverbs 18:21

When an attitude of lawlessness has set in in this way, the stage is set for the abuse of power. Moral restraints are thrown off, and the conscience is seared, because right and wrong only have relative meaning to what is right for the individual and no-one else. This is expediency and causes the truth to be thoroughly mishandled. The person who lies never has to change, because they never have to see themselves as they really are. When a person sees themselves as they really are, they see why they have to change, and they usually want to, and are grateful for the insight into themselves – '*You shall know the truth and the truth shall make you free*' (John 8:32).

But the liar is deceived about who he is and does not want to change, and so can deny any fault charged against him, as the lie has become his way of life. This ability to lie for the advantage of one's self, and for the destruction of others, is one of the most destructive forces in the earth today, and is seen at all levels of relationships, from children at school to the ambitious power mongers who seek to manipulate wealth and political power in a nation.

When is a Liar not a Liar?

In the previous chapter we asked the question, 'when is a thief not a thief?' and we saw that the scriptures showed us the process of transformation that had to take place, for the taker to become a giver. A similar process has to also take place for the transformation of a liar.

> 25. *Therefore putting away lying, each one speak truth with his neighbour, for we are members of one another.*
> 29. *Let no corrupt communication proceed out of your mouth, but what is good for necessary edification, that it may impart grace to the hearers.*   Ephesians 4:25 and 29

'I think I've really improved – I haven't said anything negative about Clive for a whole week.'

It was a counselling session again. This time only one half of the partnership was there, Alice, Clive's wife. Alice didn't think much of herself unfortunately, and couldn't understand how God could love her, and if He did, then why weren't things going better for her in her very difficult life. There was never enough money as Clive had made some bad decisions, and the kids were not 'full on' enough for the Lord, and Clive wasn't doing a thing about that either. Altogether, Alice looked at life through negative glasses. They were not the kind of spectacles that an optometrist could prescribe – they were negatively ground through unbelief. But Alice had been trying, and she hadn't said 'anything negative about Clive for one week.'

'That's only half an improvement.' I volunteered.

'No it's not. I've nearly bitten my tongue off, not saying some things I could have said.'

'Have you said anything positive about Clive?' I asked.

'Who to?'

'Anybody, Clive for a start.'

'No way. There's nothing positive to say. I suppose he tries, but nothing ever works.'

I had learned to be patient with this person. The grace of God can do wonders! I began to explain.

'You are still "bearing false witness". It's not enough to refrain from the negative talk, because good communication is to use our speech to build up. We cannot be satisfied just to come up to zero, we have to go above that line into a positive score.'

Alice gave me a 'but you don't know Clive' look. I continued to explain the principle behind good communication, and edification.

'Alice, you have not been seeing the true value and worth of Clive, the way God sees him. In many things he delivers to God the things that God requires of him, but he doesn't deliver to you the things that *you* want, and so he is of no "worth" to you.'

'How do you change that?' (Said very honestly.)

'Go to God first, and let Him show you the things He values in Clive, then start agreeing with God.'

It sounds very simple, but all true communication comes from perceiving things from the right perspective, and not from a viewpoint of self-interest. There was another step that needed taking in this situation as well – How to get Alice to value herself – And that required her to see herself as valued by God also. It all starts by asking God to show us things from His point of view. When He shows us how He loves us as we are, we can then *look at* ourselves as we really are, and being loved *in* that, can allow repentance to work in us to be changed by God into what He *really* wants us to be like.

True or False

Bearing false witness does not only involve saying things about a person that are false. It involves saying the true things about a person that are unnecessary. God knows everything about us, and covers us in His love. If God were to let everybody know every thing about us today, in full sight of everyone, all the inner self centred thoughts, desires and opinions, then life could be a very embarrassing experience. He covers us in His love and gives us opportunities to repent and change, so that He can present us blameless before Himself and others.

There will come a time however, when all the thoughts of the hearts will be made manifest before all, and that is on judgement day. In the meantime, He tells us to *'judge nothing before the time, until the Lord comes, who will both bring to light the hidden things of darkness and reveal the counsels of the hearts; and then each one's praise will come from God.'* (1 Corinthians 4:5)

One of the names for Satan is 'accuser of the brethren', and most of what he accuses us of before God, is true. But this does not make Satan a true witness. His witness is a false witness, because he accuses us for his own advantage. He thinks that by making us look bad, he can make us share the punishment and guilt for his sin. Unfortunately he succeeds in many cases, by driving people into guilt and remorse, with no hope of forgiveness. (Guilt does not drive a person to God, only *conviction*, and this comes from the Holy Spirit, not Satan.)

Therefore we must avoid following on in Satan's ministry of being the 'accuser' because we are only furthering his cause and not God's. I have seen this accusing spirit working in people, even in children, and it comes from the same source that Satan's accusing comes from, which is because of their own guilt, and the desire to make other people share in its consequences.

False witness can operate in many ways. One subtle form of false witness is *flattery*. Flattery can disguise itself as speech that edifies and builds up, but it comes from the wrong motive of self advantage and so is not giving or loving, but taking, and selfish. It is designed to manipulate favour for the flatterer by putting the one who is flattered under some kind of obligation to respond to all the 'nice things' that are being said about them. That is the misuse of power again, and is a form of misrepresentation.

Other more malicious forms of misrepresentation include, *gossiping* (the motive here being that of establishing self righteousness, either through pride or as a smoke screen for one's own attitudes and behaviour), *maligning, slandering*, and *backbiting* (for similar reasons).

Ungracious and negative talk about others is also bearing false witness, because it is communicating the same attitude of worthlessness to another person. This includes *vulgarity* (the current 'dialect' of television shows), *unnecessary bluntness, interrupting*, and *needless correcting*, and so on.

Creative Power

The creative power of the tongue and of words generally, can be seen *in the very act of creation itself, by God, when He created the world.*

> *Then God said, 'Let there be light'; and there was light.*
>   Genesis 1:3

This creative power is also seen in the maintaining of creation through the word of God.

> *Who being the brightness of His glory and the express image of His person, and upholding all things by the word of His power ...*   Hebrews 1:3

Perhaps nowhere is the significance of the power of communication seen more clearly as in the fact that Jesus Himself is called 'The Word'. If we will remember that the commandments deal primarily with *relationships* it is easy to see the importance of communication and its regulation by God, because without true communication there is no true relationship. Jesus exercised true and creative communication when He said, *'The words that I speak to you are spirit, and they are life.'*

God's Remedy for False Witness

The judgement of God upon the abuse of the truth is self deception. The person who deceives becomes progressively more deceived as he goes on, and after a while, does not know the difference between the truth and the lie. Note the warning in second Thessalonians.

> 9. *The coming of the lawless one is according to the working of Satan, with all power, signs, and lying wonders,*
> 10. *and with all unrighteous deception among those who perish, because they did not receive the love of the truth, that they might be saved.*
> 11. *And for this reason God will send them strong delusion, that they should believe the lie,*

12. *that they all may be condemned who did not believe the truth but had pleasure in unrighteousness.*

2 Thessalonians 2:9–12

The answer for the wrong heart is also found in the above scripture, in receiving a *'love of the truth'* (v. 10). This love of the truth involves a love of the truth concerning the knowledge of God, the truth of His word, and the truth about ourselves. With love for the truth working in these three different areas in our lives we will also become good communicators of truth, and be true witnesses.

Chapter 11

Enough is Enough

The Tenth Commandment

You shall not covet your neighbour's house; you shall not covet your neighbour's wife, nor his manservant, nor his maidservant, nor his ox, nor his donkey, nor anything that is your neighbour's.   Exodus 20:17

The Empty Life

We saw in the study on the last commandment, about bearing false witness, that failure to use communication for its creative purpose left open the option of using it for its destructive purpose. We saw that through 'the lie' and the bearing of false witness, worth was destroyed. The life that has no worth is unproductive – it creates and produces nothing – it is out of touch with the source of creativity and productivity, the person of God, in Jesus Christ. He is the Word of life and creation. And without receiving our daily bread from our Father through our Lord Jesus Christ we become empty.

But there must be something, somewhere, that can fill the emptiness. Where is it? It cannot come from God because faith in His provision is shipwreck. It cannot come from within because there is only emptiness in there. Then it must come from what other people have. The heart of the covetous person devours the possessions of other people and lusts after them as the source of his fulfilment. Enough is never enough because somewhere, someone has got more than they, and the covetous person must have it, whether it be wife or ox or donkey, manservant or house. Even human beings become coveted because people have become objects for gratification by now anyway.

Can you see the idolatry in this? The priests of mammon beckon the covetous person to sacrifice his integrity for more possessions. The prophets of mammon produce slicker and more appealing advertisements for the acquisition of more goods. The covetous person responds to these appeals and becomes committed with more dedication and purpose. Collections of all kinds must be amassed – artworks, ceramics, antiques, oddities, and the best of the 'world of the microchip', hi-fi and electronics, all to furnish the sanctuary of the god of mammon. It is not the possession of such things that is wrong, for they are not wrong in themselves, and can be properly appreciated for the value that they have in any culture. It is the amassing that is wrong, for the sake of finding fulfilment and identity in these things.

The covetous person has arrived at the tenth commandment and thinks he is at home there. But it is the end of a circle that has no end. Commandment number one is waiting to be met again, just around the corner – *'I am The Lord your God, you shall have no other gods before Me.'* He asks us to choose between life and death, the blessing or the curse. The last commandment, concerning false witness, left an inheritance of deception that deceived man into thinking that life fulfilment can come from a source other than God.

Rich but not Filthy Rich

It must be acknowledged and affirmed strongly though, that a person can be very wealthy, and be able to manage his wealth in a godly way without covetousness.

Abraham was one example of this, when he tithed to Melchizedek, and gave honour to God as the *'possessor of Heaven and earth'* (Genesis 14:22). Job was also a wealthy man who gave honour to God Himself as the source of his life fulfilment, and not the things that even God gives.

24. *If I have made gold my hope, or said to fine gold, 'You are my confidence';*

25. If I have rejoiced because my wealth was great, And because my hand had gained much;
26. If I have observed the sun when it shines, Or the moon moving in brightness,
27. So that my heart has been secretly enticed, and my mouth has kissed my hand;
28. This also would be an iniquity worthy of judgement, for I would have denied God who is above.

Job 31:24–28

There is no deception here – no sense of injustice that God owed Job his wealth. Job knew that the Lord was the one who gave and the one who took away. It is clear in the word of God that it is God who makes people wealthy anyway (unless they gain their wealth illegally, in which case they lose everything else. (Proverbs 13:11.)

> *'And you shall remember The Lord your God, for it is He who gives you power to get wealth ...'*
> Deuteronomy 8:18

There is a principle in scripture that shows that God will even transfer wealth from those who should *not* have it to those whom He thinks should have it.

> *A good man leaves an inheritance to his children's children. But the wealth of the sinner is stored up for the righteous.*
> Proverbs 13:22

> *Then you shall see and become radiant, and your heart shall swell with joy; because the abundance of the sea shall be turned to you, the wealth of the Gentiles shall come to you.*
> Isaiah 60:5

If these principles are true then the Christian should have great hope to 'enjoy his labour under the sun', and be willing to work with the hope that God is his real source of provision, but that He will use man to be His channel of supply. This is a motivation to have faith in God and not to covet what other people have.

Socialism – You Owe Me

Socialism appears to be based on an unselfish motive of the just and equal redistribution of wealth, with the state being the sovereign benefactor and custodian of all property, so that there is no personal inheritance or personal freedom to acquire wealth. This is aimed at removing the greed motive and the misuse of birthright, status, or special ability that would take from others and advantage onself.

It is patently obvious that this experiment with God's property has failed, because the real motive is not unselfish at all but a covetous reaction to what the wealthy have, even though the wealthy may be misusing God's property also, to their advantage. The answer however, is not socialism, or communism, but a biblical response to the eighth commandment, which turns the taker into a giver, releasing productivity and liberality for the blessing of others and to the honour and glory of God.

Socialism redistributes the wealth, it is true, but in fact what it redistributes is poverty! This is because the worth and true value of a person and their labour and hire is not appreciated, and true scriptural principles of inheritance cannot be applied. With this depreciation of worth and incentive, there also comes the abuse of the power in the hands of the bureaucracy that manages the property and opportunity of the masses. The power base that is built is totally atheistic, and in fact is taking for itself the place of God as the 'possessor of Heaven and earth'.

Lucifer was the first socialist. He coveted God's place of power and glory, and felt that he deserved to have the inheritance due to God's son Jesus, an inheritance which Jesus shares willingly with His church (Which is why Satan hates the Church so much). The following scripture from Isaiah demonstrates the determination of Lucifer to follow through with his plan of revolution, in which he somehow must have persuaded the other fallen angels who went with him, that they would get their fair share of the new order of things. What he got in fact, was destruction and a final judgement of being cast down to Hell. Some form of destruction, whether it be physical, financial, emotional, or spiritual, is the judgement of God upon the covetous person. This is because covetousness is as idolatry

(Colossians 3:5), and God's judgement upon idolatry is the destruction of idols.

> 12. *How you are fallen from Heaven, O Lucifer, son of the morning! How you are cut down to the ground, you who weakened the nations!*
> 13. *For you have said in your heart: 'I will ascend into Heaven, I will exalt my throne above the stars of God; I will also sit on the mount of the congregation on the farthest sides of the north;*
> 14. *I will ascend above the heights of the clouds, I will be like The Most High.'*
> 15. *Yet you shall be brought down to Sheol, to the lowest depths of the pit.*   Isaiah 14:12–15

Socialism does away with true inheritance as a principle and seeks to enforce its own form of social and material justice and equality. The 'you owe me' mentality however, puts socialism in the category of taking and not giving, and denies that God owns everything.

Window Shopping for Identity

Window shopping is different to ordinary shopping, mainly because it doesn't cost anything. We can wander through the arcades and look into the shop windows at what we want, without having to commit ourselves to any sacrifice. But there is a danger, because the more we look, the more we may want to have, and that is when covetousness can lead to financial destruction.

In a similar way we can window shop for some kind of an image that we want for ourselves. The place we go to though, is not a shopping arcade to look into shop windows, but into people's lives that we want to emulate. Emulation is branded as one of the works of the flesh in Galatians chapter five and verse twenty, and in the New King James Bible it is translated jealousy. This is the act of coveting the identity of another person.

This is the ultimate act of self rejection and idolatry, and so shows to us how close this commandment is to commandment number two, about the making of images and idolatry. This was pointed out in the beginning of the book, when we were considering the cyclic nature of the ten commandments, and that when we came around to commandment number ten we would find that it was similar in nature to the commandment that was immediately on the *other side* of the first commandment.

There are two ways in which this personal covetousness, envy, or jealousy can operate. One expression is the direct focus upon the identity of another person, and seeking to copy their way of dress or speech or manner. In this way a person is drawing their sense of 'being' from the attributes of another person. This may cause no direct harm or offence to the person being copied at all, and in fact the person being copied may not even know, and if they do know, may even be flattered. The one that suffers is the one doing the copying, or emulating, because of the emptiness and discontent in their lives.

The other expression of personal covetousness however, is more destructive, and causes damage to the person being emulated as well. This kind of covetousness seeks to consume the identity of another person by taking their friends or even their spouse. This comes from the sin of people comparing themselves with others and desiring the success or attributes they possess. Paul warns of this in his letter to the Corinthians.

> ... *But they, measuring themselves by themselves, and comparing themselves among themselves, are not wise.*
> 2 Corinthians 10:12

Much competition between God's people in church and between churches is a result of this flaw and failure in people's lives.

The Remedy

God's remedy for all kinds of covetousness is twofold. He destroys the false sense of identity that has been established by taking it away from a person. There are many ways in which

God does this. It can be through their sin or foolishness which brings shame or ruin upon them, or He will cause their efforts to eventually fail. The second thing that God does is make available a revelation of His grace, and the contentment that can be ours by accepting godliness instead of worldliness for our fulfilment.

> 6. *But godliness with contentment is great gain.*
> 7. *For we brought nothing into this world, and it is certain we can carry nothing out.*　　　　　　　1 Timothy 6:6–7

A great encouragement and exhortation to safeguard us against being covetous is found in Psalm thirty-seven.

> 1. *Do not fret because of evildoers, Nor be envious of the workers of iniquity.*
> 9. *For evildoers shall be cut off; But those who wait on the Lord, They shall inherit the earth.*　　　　　　　Psalm 37:1, 9

Living in the grace of God is living free from the concept of what *is deserved*. Grace does not seek justice for itself or demand its rights. There is the contentment that God wants us to have in Jesus Christ, and this of course leads us right around again to the challenge of the first commandment, that from Him, and to Him and through Him are all things. In fact, it would be beneficial, having just finished this last chapter, to read again the chapter which deals with the first commandment. Then you can put the book down!